The Duns Branch

Leighton Buzzard - Dunstable - Luton

by Bill Simpson

Lamplight Publications

Published by Lamplight Publications
260 Colwell Drive, Witney, Oxfordshire OX8 7LW
and 38 Spinney Drive,
Banbury, Oxfordshire OX16 9TA

First published 1998

Reprographics by Original Repro Limited
Unit C, Southfield Road
Eynsham, Oxon OX8 1JD
Printed and bound at the Alden Press

Acknowledgements

The author would like to gratefully acknowledge the support of the following who have been so generous in their efforts in helping to produce this history.
Bob Berry, Ian Bowley, F Cockman,
Maurice Conquest, Rod Dingwall, Fred Frazer,
Fred Hobbs, Colin Holmes,
Christopher Hunt *Imperial War Museum*,
M King *Leighton Buzzard Observer*,
Kevin Lane, *LNWR Society*,
Monica Povey *Leighton Buzzard Library*,
Mr M Rudd, Mr F Parkinson, Mr C Pepper,
John Sharland *Southill Collection*,
William Shelford *Archivist LBNGR*, Bert Smith,
Stephen Summerson,
Nigel Lutt *Bedford County Records*,
Buckinghamshire County Records,
The late Geoff Webb, Alan Willmott.

Webb 'Coal Tank' pauses with a train from Dunstable at
Stanbridgeford in LNWR days, note LNWR coach
and signal
LNWR Society

Contents

River, canal and railway at Linslade
Colin Holmes Collection

Foreword

The Dunstable Branch only remained in the typical junction to terminus form for ten years. With the opening of the line through to Luton in 1858 it became for all intents and purposes a through connecting route to that town and subsequently Hatfield, Welwyn and beyond. The title therefore may seem to be a misnomer in that sense but from the point of view of the ownership of the line by the London & North Western Railway and the later London Midland & Scottish Railway it remained as a branch. The Great Northern Railway and London & North Eastern Railway owned the extended section from Dunstable onwards. Nevertheless for the convenience of the historical scope of this book it is this first section that requires focus with its intense use of loads from the heavy ground works of sand and chalk. This lifts it out of the bucolic mould of a country branch line into an intensity of operations requiring much organisation and dedication from its railway staff.

As the 'Dunstable Dasher' or the extended 'Skimpot Flyer' progressed with their daily run of passengers the heavy freight locomotives would pass alongside on this double track line, toiling up Sewell Bank, or, with the protesting squeal of brakes try to hold trains to fifteen miles per hour on the descent. It was all part of a time when railways were more of an adventure than they are today. When their control was vested in the skill, strength and judgement of the men who worked them.

Bill Simpson 1998

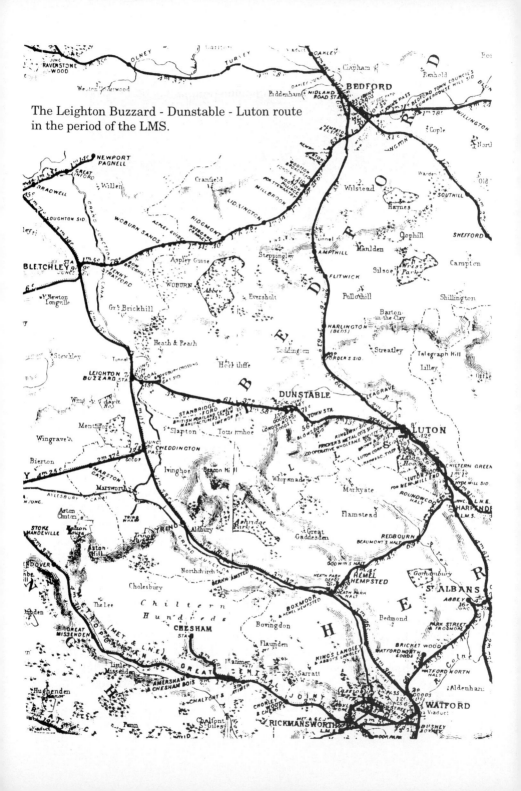

The Leighton Buzzard - Dunstable - Luton route
in the period of the LMS.

This station building is believed to be from the original
station at Leighton, here situated in some garden setting
Bedfordshire & Luton Archives & Records Service

CHAPTER ONE

Early History

Had the first plan for the London & Birmingham Railway to pass
west of the district, going through Buckingham and avoiding the
area altogether been acted upon it would have caused a much
longer extended branch for the Dunstable Railway to build. The
hostility of the first Duke of Buckingham in blocking this plan
ensured that the prospect was made easier by forcing the line east
through Linslade. When at last the line opened from Euston to
Denbigh Hall on April 9, 1838, a station was opened at Linslade,
quarter of a mile or so south of the tunnel which was 286 yards
through the blue clay and iron sandstone. In 1845 there were two
schemes to serve Dunstable by rail. As the town is situated on
what is now the A5 the main route to Holyhead it had special
importance. The local inn, 'The Sugar Loaf' was a staging post
for the Irish Mail coach providing refreshment for passengers
and changing the horses. One of the schemes for rail connection
was the Cambridge & Oxford Railway to be engineered by Joseph
Lock. This would have run through to Luton, Dunstable, Totternhoe, Eaton Bray, Cheddington, along the Aylesbury branch of the
L&B railway to carry on to Oxford. This scheme met with opposition in the House of Lords and was eventually truncated to serv-

ing Royston and Hitchin only, opened on October 21, 1850 which was in fact later than the eventual Dunstable Railway.

Another scheme was put forward by George Stephenson with his son Robert who wished to connect the burgeoning industrial town of Luton with the the L&BR by extending the then proposed Dunstable Railway. Luton was becoming a concentration of industry with its straw plait hats and boxes, many of its coal requirements were awkwardly brought over land from the Grand Junction Canal. To this purpose George Stephenson attended a meeting at the George Hotel, Luton on May 11, 1844 and told his audience that he would give them a railway. The plan to place Luton at the end of a long branch was not received with enthusiasm, a great deal of rancour was expressed and the meeting ended in bitterness, enough for Stephenson to say that he would never visit the place again. He never did. The prospectus for the Dunstable Branch Railway (1844) states that the capital shall be £50,000 raised in 2,500 shares of £20 each, with powers to borrow on consent of the L&BR a further £16,600 when all the £50,000 capital has been paid up. The Engineer is to be George Stephenson and the Committee will consist of local luminaries, Richard Gutteridge (land owner and lawyer) Benjamin Bennet (brewer), Henry Goude, John Cooper and nine others. Two Directors were being appointed from the L&BR Ross Donnelly Mangies and Thomas Young. The advantages of the arrival of the railway are expressed for the straw plait industry and the cheaper prices for coal, coke and timber. Not forgetting of course one industry that would have important prospects for the railway, the Totternhoe stone quarries. The Contractor for the line was one T Jackson.

The railway was described as starting from Dunstable through the parishes of Sewell, Houghton Regis, Totternhoe, Tatnall, Tilsworth, Eaton Bray, Stanbridge, Eggington, Billington and Linslade. A clause was inserted stringently protecting the structure and free usage of the Grand Junction canal over which it would pass near Leighton.

From the outset the L&BR had a strong hand in the affairs of the line; they supplied locomotives and rolling stock on a list of tolls and purchased additional lands alongside which they rented for the use of the Dunstable Railway. The tolls read as follows: coal, iron in pigs and rods, salt, dung, compost. manure, lime and limestone; also materials for the repair of public roads; all charged at three farthings per ton per mile.

For coke, culm, charcoal, cinders, stones for building, pitching and paving, bricks, tiles, slates, clay, sand, wrought iron and iron castings, soda, oil cake, oil in cakes, pitch, tar, saltpetre, ale and beer, raw hides, hoofs and horns, bones, asphaltum, sugar, coffee, rice, tallow, cheese, butter in casks, potatoes, grain, corn, flour, hides, dyewoods, earthenware, timber, stones, and deals, metals (except iron), nails, anvils, vices, chains; charged at one penny per ton per mile; if required to go in covered carriages an additional halfpenny per mile.

For all manufactured iron, steel tools, metals (not iron), bark, Manchester packs, linen, paper, hay and straw; charged two pence per ton per mile.

For cotton, wool, drugs, manufactured goods, silk, fruit, fish, furniture; two and a halfpence per ton per mile.

With regard to cattle it was for every ox, bull in own carriage one penny per mile; in a company carriage an extra half pence per mile. For calf, pig, sheep, lamb in own carriage half pence per mile; in company carriage extra farthing per mile.

For running vehicles on the line, for every carriage under one ton three pence per mile; for every additional quarter ton an extra penny. Hired from the L&BR it would cost an additional half pence per mile.

The toll for locomotives was one penny per mile for each passenger or animal and for each ton of goods.

Each passenger was allowed to take in luggage 110lbs first class and 60lbs for second class with no extra charge. The toll charge for the passenger was 1st class three pence per mile, 2nd class two pence per mile, 3rd class half a pence per mile.

Horses were five pence per mile, cattle two pence per mile, sheep and small animals three farthings per mile. A carriage without passengers was seven pence per mile, with passengers five pence per mile. To hire a wagon to carry six oxen or twenty-five sheep six pence per mile.

The Bill for the London & Birmingham & Dunstable Railway was successful and became an Act on June 30, 1845. In the interim period the London & Birmingham Railway became part of the London & North Western Railway in June 1846 and this larger company adopted the support for the railway from the former. A striking difference however between the two companies was in the building of the line. The survey carried out by the L&BR included a gradient just under a mile of 1 in 27! This climb to Dunstable would prohibit steam locomotives and, in the same manner as the first Euston station to Camden, was to be worked by rope incline. The LNWR modified this survey and extended the gradient to just over a mile at the stiff but more agreeable incline of 1 in 40 and dispensed with the cable working plan.

Another proposal that failed was for a twenty mile extension of the Dunstable Railway with a branch to run from Watford to Luton and thence to Dunstable in 1845. The scheme did not find favour and was rejected in the House of Commons.

An interesting feature of the Dunstable Railway survey was at 4½ furlongs from the main line where it was proposed to raise a tramway that ran from the canal to the road by 3ft 6in in order to cross over it. This was in fact a connection to the coal depot on the Mentmore Road south of Linslade. When the railway was opened it replaced the use of the tramway with the opening of Ledburn Wharf to supply the coal depot alongside the line with sidings. The depot was owned by Clay Cross Collieries, the proprietors of this concern being no less than George and Robert Stephenson, George Carr Glyn, Chairman of the LNWR, Joseph Saunders, Joshua Walmsley and subsequently the notorious George Hudson of Eastern Counties and Great Eastern Railways. When the branch to Dunstable was built the railway ran at the back of the coal depot, closer than the canal, which was a neat advantage of the survey. In the period before 'block' signalling on the branch the crossing was called 'Ledburn Gates' with the attendant crossing keeper's house alongside; this changed to Ledburn Crossing by 1884 just before 'block' working was introduced. The branch was the last on the LNWR to work on the time interval system as it was converted to absolute block on January 18, 1886.

At 4¾ furlongs the railway passed over the River Ouzel which is the border of Buckinghamshire and Bedfordshire. Here the River and canal are pinched closely together allowing them to be spanned by an extensive bridge, probably of cast and wrought iron and timber that was later rebuilt in steel.

A modification from this original survey was the climb up Sewell Bank which had been surveyed with a gradient of a staggering 1 in 27. This climb would have been a formidable barrier to locomotive use on the line, let alone descending brake power! This was planned to commence at a point 5 miles and two chains from Leighton and terminate at 5 miles 71 chains, about half a mile in length. This would have created a cutting with the greatest height of embankment being 28ft 6inches and greatest depth being 31ft. The vertical rise would have been 168ft compared to the one as built on the 1 in 40 incline being 165ft.

All of this endeavour must have been witnessed with curiosity and foreboding by the tenant of Sewell Farm very close to the workings at that point, one Elizabeth Cook.

Happily all went ahead as planned and the Dunstable Railway could announce their line open for business from May 29 for goods and for passengers on June 1, 1848, with the trains run by the LNWR. In all probability those early trains would be of four-wheel coaches with one of the bar framed Bury engines at the head with its 'haystack' firebox polished and glinting in the summer sunlight and its tall chimney drifting smoke and steam along the smart green and black coaches.

The branch from Leighton Buzzard to Dunstable achieved some reputation throughout its long lifetime. It was built over the rising ground of the Chilterns with uncompromising gradients; one mentioned of 1 in 40 for 1 mile. To add further to its reputation it secured some of the heaviest traffic with chalk and sand trains. For a modest branch line it was no easy option for the engines and men to amble back and forth with the the the daily shuttle of a push-pull engine and two coaches, or a local pick-up daily goods train. It had such workings like any other, but the freight working was quite another matter. The town of Dunstable is about 500 feet above sea level and Leighton Buzzard about 300 feet; obviously in such a short distance some severe gradients would be encountered. Approaching from Leighton the daunting rise was always visible and started to become apparent at Gower's Siding when the gradient steepened to 1 in 40 with a short run, less than half a mile, before the terminus; this was called Sewell Bank after the nearby village. This gradient was a severe test for the comparatively large 2-6-2 tank engines of the 1950's with two coaches which merits praise for both engines and men of the LNWR managing with the tiny 2-4-2 tank engines. Another difficulty was the sharp curve approaching Leighton Buzzard station from Grovebury Crossing and up a gradient of 1 in 80. After a short climb over the canal, the line dropped down, then quickly began the climb to the station. One of the worst prospects for a crew with a full train of 1,000 or so tons of chalk was to be halted at Grovebury Crossing, the restart would rattle windows across Leighton and Linslade.

The situation at Luton that had so aggrieved George Stephenson could not be left in isolation as far as the railways were concerned, Luton was far too important a town for railway promoters to leave aside. This time came the involvement of the Great Northern Railway (1846). A line was subsequently built from

Hatfield and Welwyn to Luton and on to Dunstable to connect with the LNWR and the west coast main line. This was the Luton, Dunstable & Welwyn Junction Railway that had been formed in 1854 as the branch was being built. This apparent extension to the route was authorised on July 16, 1855 to build the line from Dunstable to Luton and Welwyn. This section of the route was opened to goods on April 5, 1858 and for passengers on May 3, 1858. Parliament refused to sanction a crossing on the Holyhead Road at Dunstable between the two railways; concluding that such an important road could not be made subservient to the railway. The road would have to be crossed by a bridge. On June 28, 1858 this latter Company was amalgamated with the Hertford & Welwyn Junction Company and the combined undertaking was known as the Hertford, Luton & Dunstable Railway. After some protracted wrangling this Railway was purchased by the Great Northern Railway in 1861, which effectively had a route from its main line to Dunstable from Welwyn when it was opened on September 1, 1860. Both the branches from Dunstable and Hertford being extended alongside the main line into Hatfield which is 20 1/4 miles away from Dunstable North.

From the opening of the Luton - Dunstable section in 1858 the LNWR ran Luton trains until the Luton - Welwyn section was opened on September 1, 1860

Up until October 1, 1860 the Luton trains had to reverse into the Dunstable terminus of the LNWR. On that date a new station was opened called Dunstable Church Street after negotiations between the two companies for a joint station had failed. Later the GNR offered to rebuild Dunstable GNR (Church Street) station to be used also by the LNWR. The LNWR required it to be a joint venture with equal rights; the GNR did not find this acceptable. A new LNWR station was opened in January 1866 on the main running line and the former station site became a goods yard. Up until then through trains calling at the LNWR station had awkward reversals which must have disadvantaged train times. Both stations were eventually renamed, Dunstable Church Street became Dunstable Town on January 1, 1927, whilst the Dunstable of the LNWR became Dunstable North on September 25, 1950.

The LNWR who took over the Dunstable Railway operations from the L&BR had an agreeable working relationship with the GNR who enlarged the Luton station and added an island platform. To this the LNWR worked trains between Leighton and Luton from April 1, 1881. On May 1, 1883, a service was introduced to work from Luton to Dunstable, Leighton, and Bletchley but this was somewhat short lived and on November 1, 1884 the trains ran only to Leighton Buzzard again. This continued until after World War Two when road competition meant that it was no longer viable. The LNWR introduced block working and inter-locking signalling in 1886.

In 1886 the LNWR decide to centralise all the local workshop requirements at Bletchley which was by that time a major operational centre from which all the branches radiated out. Removing the carpenters' shop and other smaller service areas meant that forty families had to leave Leighton and Linslade district and relocate. This caused a great deal of bitterness amongst local tradesmen. Staple goods traffic on the line tended to be lime from Forders at Tottenhoe to Leighton Buzzard; coal to Dunstable Gas Works; sand from Grovebury Sidings and a great deal of agricultural produce. Also, flowers and fruit loaded at Stanbridgeford from Wallaces's at Eaton Bray.

The war was taking its toll in 1917 when the LNWR instructed that no trains from Euston should stop at Leighton between 11.00am and 2.40pm. In the Control system of working which was needed to administer the heavy traffic of the war, Bletchley became responsible for the lines just north of Tring to a point just south of Roade. The war had few benefits, but there was one for the trade around Leighton, when cheap sand from the ballast of ships ceased to enter the country. The existing pits in the district as a result were given a tremendous boost to their supply demands for local sand to be described in the chapter on the LBNGR.

Timetable July 1890

Euston dep	6.00	8.00	9.30	10.15	11.45	15.15	18.00	19.10
Leighton arr	7.57	9.30	10.27	12.20	14.45	16.45	19.15	21.35
Standbridgeford	8.06	Sig	10.37	Sig	Sig	Sig	Sig	Sig
Dunstable arr	8.12	9.45	10.44	12.35	15.00	17.00	19.30	21.50
Dunstable dep	7.25	9.00	10.05	11.23	13.28	15.05	18.05	20.20
Stanbridgeford	7.32	9.05	10.10	11.30	13.34	15.10	18.12	20.27
Leighton arr	7.42	9.15	10.20	11.40	13.43	15.20	18.22	20.37
Euston arr	9.35	10.25		13.55	16.10	17.25	19.35	23.15

Note: 'Sig' means that passengers travelling by down trains must inform the Guard that they wish to alight at Stanbridgeford, and intending passengers must give a clear signal to the driver. Presumably this was to give a clear run at the Sewell bank when possible.

Dunstable LNWR post 1866 station which was built for through running to Luton and the Great Northern lines. Two staggered platforms were arranged and the Great Northern train is awaiting to depart from the opposite platform.The locomotive is J6 no 364 0-6-0 Stirling goods engine which it appears is exceptionally being used for passenger work. The platform in the foreground being for Leighton bound trains. The local service to Leighton can be faintly seen in the bay with the engine, that looks like a small tank, behind the signal.
Mr F Banfield

OPPOSITE PAGE:Wing Crossing of unknown date with smartly dressed crossing keeper. The signalling appartus is not LNWR and may therefore date from the early period when Saxby & Farmer Co supplied signalling machinery to the Company. The Crossing keeper's house is interesting as the half timbered style is identically related to the buildings of the Bedford Railway (Bletchley - Bedford 1846). This is due to the contractor for them a Mr T Jackson using the same architect who remains unknown.
Bob Berry Collection

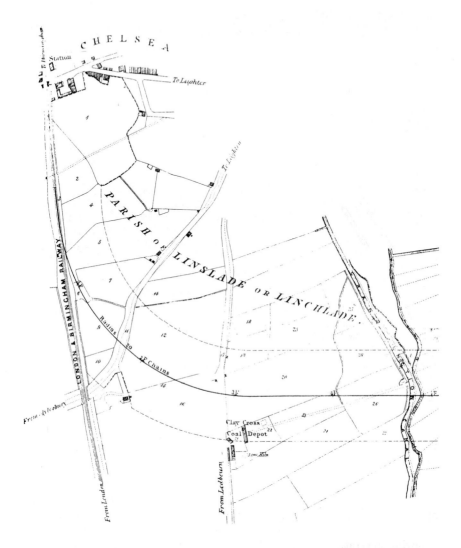

Plans of the first survey for the railway from the London & Birmingham
Railway at Linslade to Dunstable. The junction station is on the original
site with the crossing alongside it. Note also Clay Cross Colliery Depot
and the railway survey crossing a pair of dotted lines leading to the canal,
this was the tramway that connected with the Grand Junction Canal for
coal imports. With the building of the railway sidings would be put in
replacing this tramway, being called, appropriate to the canal - Ledburn
Wharf, remaining as coal sidings until the last days of the line.
Bedfordshire & Luton Archives & Records Service

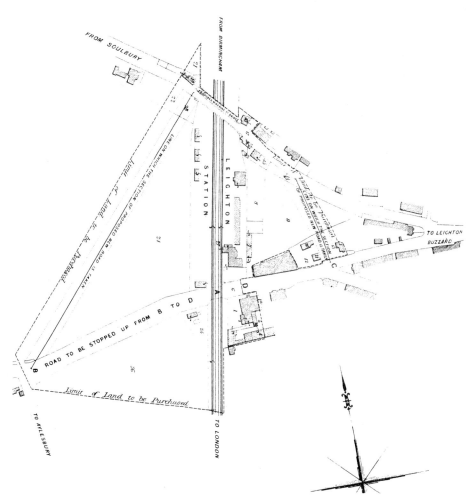

Plans drawn up by the LNWR to provide space for the new goods relief line being built from Bletchley to Primrose Hill Tunnel. This involved removing the station from north to south of the road to Aylesbury, and closing the road and crossing completely. To provide alternatives they had to build Springfield Road, widening the bridge on the road to Soulbury to allow two horse drawn carts to pass and put in another link road between the Soulbury Road and the approach to the new station. A new pedestrain footbridge over the station would retain the right of way, the crossing now being displaced.The Station Hotel would now have its back to the station. *Bucks County Record Office, ref P / UC114*

Stanbridgeford the only station between Leighton Buzzard and Dunstable it appears to have developed gradually from 1849. The siding on the left dates from the earliest days as a siding for separating the trains prior to ascending Sewell bank which can be seen in the distance.
Ian Bowley

Leighton Buzzard station 1859 structure. With rebuilding the stations
along the line began to look more permanent and as secure as other public
buildings; thus this imposing frontage with arched windows and entrance
doorway. It was re-roofed in 1957 and with later electrification some
demolition began in 1962, until complete rebuilding in 1989.
Colin Holmes

Fourth loop line built on this side of station. Tunnel had
three bores, fourth to be made with new line

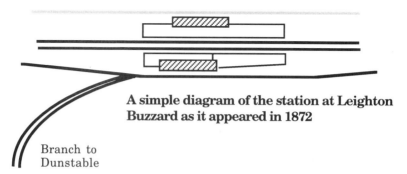

**A simple diagram of the station at Leighton
Buzzard as it appeared in 1872**

Branch to
Dunstable

A simplified diagram of the station of Leighton Buzzard in 1872 as plans
for the fourth loop line were drawn up.
Bill Simpson

19

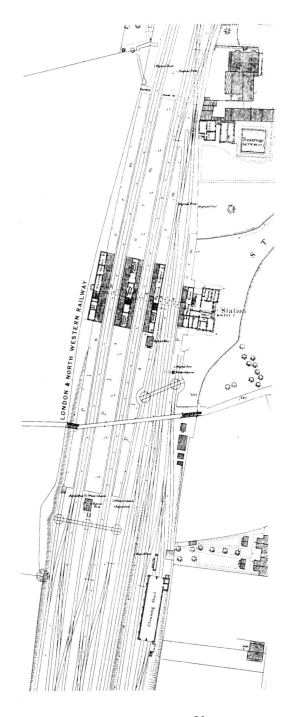

Leighton Buzzard station in 1880 after the construction of the final through line of 1876. Most of the development around the station had not occurred by this time but the roads had been changed as a result of the 1857 plans of the railway. Note extreme right the road leading to the railway then ending, this was the original road to Aylesbury that was closed, alongside it the imposing station hotel, now with its back to the railway. The cast and wrought iron footbridge is in situ to retain the right of pedestrians access to the opposite side protected by agreement with the London & Birmingham Railway and existing to the present.
Ordnance Survey/Leighton Buzzard Library

THE DUNSTABLE BRANCH OF THE LNWR

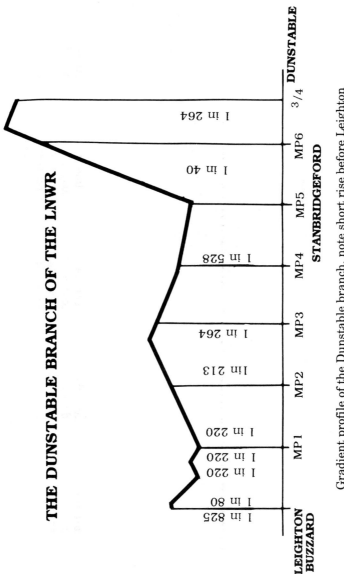

Gradient profile of the Dunstable branch, note short rise before Leighton station to cross river and canal.
Drawn by Robert Simpson.

21

Class 8F no 48445 at the north end of Leighton Buzzard station, looking south on the 25 May, 1962. The bridge above was widened by the LNWR in 1858 for road access after closing down the station crossing. The goods shed seen through the bridge is on the site of the original station.
Peter E Baughan

OPPOSITE PAGE: Billington Road Crossing during the first world war period before the opening of the narrow gauge railway in 1919.
The photograph reveals clearly the dreadful condition of the roads caused by the movement of such high tonnages of sand. Note the characteristically tall semaphores of the LNWR protecting the crossing. Also the Great Central Railway wagon on the right.
Bedfordshire & Luton Archives & Record Service

DUNSTABLE BRANCH.—WEEK DAYS.

Working timetable for 1902. Second class fares were withdrawn from Aylesbury, Luton, Dunstable, Newport Pagnell branches on January 10, 1911.

P R H Webber Collection

LONDON AND BIRMINGHAM RAILWAY.

COACHING DEPARTMENT.

HOURS OF DEPARTURE AND TIME TABLE.

(On and after Thursday, 20th June 1839.)

DOWN TRAINS from LONDON.

TRAINS.	DEPARTURE FROM LONDON.	HARROW.	WATFORD.	BOX MOOR.	BERKHAMP.	TRING.	LEIGHTON.	BLETCHLEY.	WOLVERTON.	ROADE.	BLISWORTH.	WEEDON.	CRICK.	RUGBY.	BRANDON.	COVENTRY.	HAMPTON.	ARRIVAL AT BIRMINGHAM.
* MIXED Calling at ... Class *	6 a.m.	—	6.45	—	—	7.25	—	—	8.15	—	8.50	9. 5	—	9.10	—	10.10	—	11 a.m.
* MIXED	— a.m.	8.30	8.50	9.10	9.20	9.35	10. 0	10.15	10.30	10.55	11. 5	11.35	11.45	12. 5	12.20	12.35	1. 0	1¼ p.m.
* MAIL	9 a.m.	—	—	—	10.4m	—	—	—	11.41	—	—	12.28	—	—	1.36	—	—	2¼ p.m.
* MIXED Calling at 1st Class Stations	11 a.m.	—	11.1	—	—	12.25	12.50	—	1.15	—	1.50	2. 5	—	2.10	—	3.10	—	4 p.m.
MIXED	2 p.m.	2.30	2.50	4.10	3.20	3.35	4. 0	4.15	4.30	4.55	5. 5	5.35	5.45	6. 5	6.20	6.35	7. 0	7¼ p.m.
MIXED To Wolverton.	5 p.m.	5.30	5.50	6.10	6.20	6.35	7. 0	7.15	7.30	—	—	—	—	—	—	—	—	—
FIRST	7 p.m.	—	7.45	—	—	8.25	—	—	9.15	—	9.50	10. 5	—	10.10	—	11.10	—	12 p.m.
* MAIL Mixed	8¼ p.m.	—	—	—	—	9.56	—	—	10.54	—	—	11.50	—	—	1. 0	—	—	2 a.m.

N.B. The 8 a.m. 2 p.m. and 5 p.m. Trains will call at the Aylesbury Junction.

SUNDAY TRAINS.

TRAINS.																		
MIXED	8 a.m.	8.30	8.50	9.10	9.20	9.35	10. 0	10.15	10.30	10.55	11. 5	11.35	11.45	12. 5	12.20	12.35	1. 0	1¼ p.m.
* MAIL	9¼ a.m.	—	—	—	—	10.4m	—	—	11.41	—	—	12.33	—	—	1.36	—	—	2¼ p.m.
MIXED To Wolverton.	5 p.m.	5.30	5.50	6.10	6.20	6.35	7. 0	7.15	7.30	—	—	—	—	—	—	—	—	—
* MAIL, Mixed	8¼ p.m.	—	—	—	—	9.56	—	—	10.54	—	—	11.50	—	—	1. 0	—	—	2 a.m.

UP TRAINS from BIRMINGHAM.

TRAINS.	DEPARTURE FROM BIRMINGHAM	HAMPTON.	COVENTRY.	BRANDON.	RUGBY.	CRICK.	WEEDON.	BLISWORTH.	ROADE.	WOLVERTON.	BLETCHLEY.	LEIGHTON.	TRING.	BERKHAMP.	BOX MOOR.	WATFORD.	HARROW.	ARRIVAL AT LONDON.
MIXED From Wolverton	—	—	—	—	—	—	—	—	6.45	7. 5	7.20	7.45	7.55	8. 5	8.30	8.45	—	9¼ a.m.
MIXED	6 a.m.	6.35	6.50	7. 5	7.25	7.50	8. 5	8.25	8.40	9. 0	9.20	9.35	10. 0	10.10	10.30	10.35	11. 0	11¼ a.m.
* MAIL	8¼ a.m.	—	9.17	—	—	—	10.36	—	—	11.11	—	—	12.11	—	—	—	—	1¼ p.m.
* MIXED	12 noon	12.25	12.50	1. 5	1.25	1.50	2. 5	2.25	2.40	3. 0	3.20	3.35	4. 0	4.10	4.20	4.35	5. 0	5¼ p.m.
* MIXED	1¼ p.m.	1.40	2. 5	2.20	2.40	3. 5	3.20	3.40	3.55	4.15	4.35	4.50	5.15	5.25	5.35	5.50	6.15	6¾ p.m.
* FIRST	3¼ p.m.	—	4.15	—	4.45	—	5.25	5.45	—	6.10	—	6.45	7.10	—	—	7.40	—	8¼ p.m.
MIXED	5 p.m.	5.35	5.50	6. 5	6.25	6.50	7. 5	7.25	7.40	8. 0	8.20	8.35	9. 0	9.10	9.20	9.35	10. 0	10¼ p.m.
* MAIL, Mixed	12 p.m.	—	12.53	—	—	—	2. 9	—	—	2.58	—	—	4. 3	—	—	—	—	5¼ a.m.

N.B. The 6¼ a.m. 6 a.m. and 2½ p.m. Trains will call at the Aylesbury Junction.

SUNDAY TRAINS.

TRAINS.																		
MIXED From Wolverton	—	—	—	—	—	—	—	—	6.45	7. 5	7.20	7.45	7.55	8. 5	8.30	8.45	—	9¼ a.m.
* MAIL	8¼ a.m.	—	9.17	—	—	—	10.36	—	—	11.11	—	—	12.11	—	—	—	—	1¼ p.m.
* MIXED	1¼ p.m.	1.55	2.20	2.25	2.55	2.30	3.25	3.55	4.10	4.30	4.50	5. 5	5.20	5.40	5.50	6. 5	6.20	7 p.m.
* MAIL, Mixed	12 p.m.	—	12.53	—	—	—	2. 9	—	—	2.58	—	—	4. 3	—	—	—	—	5¼ a.m.

N.B.—The times of the Trains conveying the Mails are fixed by the Postmaster General, under the powers granted by act of Parliament, Act 1 & 2 Vic. cap. 98.

Private Carriages and Horses must be at the Stations at least 15 minutes before the time of departure, and none will be taken by the night Mail Trains.

The Company strongly recommend all Passengers to have their name and destination clearly stated on their luggage, and to see that it is put upon the carriages.

The Trains marked with an asterisk, are in conjunction with those of the Grand Junction Railway, sufficient time being allowed at the Birmingham Station, where refreshments are provided, and waiting rooms, with a female attendant.

June, 1839.

HOWSON, Printer, Barbican.

Trains of the London & Birmingham Railway in June 1839 including Leighton station.
Ron Miller Collection

Linslade Tunnel with 45375 emerging on the 17 of August 1958. The track on which the engine is running was built as a result of the construction of the goods relief line in 1859. The centre bore of course being constructed for the original main line by the London & Birmingham Railway. The west bore, with its very restricted clearance is not visible, this was opened for the new loop line in 1876.
K Barrow

TO DUNSTABLE, LUTON, & GREAT NORTHERN.

																Sun.	Sun.
LEIGHTON L. & N.W.	...	8 25	9 30	9 45	10 28	12 10	2 00	...	6 0	7 10	9 15					
Dunstable ....arr.	...	8 40	9 45	10 0	10 43	12 25	3 5	...	6 20	7 25	9 30					
„ ....dep.	7 50	9 15	...	10 45	...	1 0	3 30	4 40	7 0	...	10 0	...	6 15			
„ Church St. G. N.	7 55	9 20	...	10 49	...	1 5	3 35	4 45	7 5	...	10 5	...	6 20			
Luton ....arr.	8 5	9 30	...	10 57	..	1 15	3 45	4 55	7 15	...	10 15	...	6 30			
„ ....dep.	8 10	9 35	...	11 0	...	1 18	3 51	4 58	7 21	...	...	7 35	6 33			
Harpenden ......„......	8 22	9 47	...	11 15	...	1 30	4 3	5 10	7 35	...	...	7 50	6 50			
Wheathampstead	8 29	9 54	...	11 22	...	1 37	4 8	5 15	7 42	...	...	8 0	7 0			
Hatfield	8 45	10 13	...	11 37	...	1 55	4 26	5 33	7 58	...	...	8 17	7 20			
Kings Cross	9 32	10 50	...	12 30	...	2 55	5 35	6 45	9 5	...		9 45	8 45			

GREAT NORTHERN TO LUTON, DUNSTABLE, &c.

Kings Cross, G. N.	...	...	7 55	9 25	11 10	...	2 45	...	5 5	6 0	8 0	7 30	8 0			
Hatfield	...	...	8 52	10 20	12 0	...	3 15	...	5 47	6 45	5 50	8 45	8 50			
Wheathampstead	...	...	9 7	10 38	12 15	...	3 30	...	6 4	7 0	9 5	9 0	9 5			
Harpenden	...	...	9 15	10 41	12 24	...	3 35	...	6 11	7 6	9 11	9 7	9 14			
Luton ....arr.	...	..	9 30	10 55	12 35	...	3 50	...	6 25	7 20	9 27	9 23	9 32			
„ ....dep.	7 0	8 30	9 35	10 58	12 38	1 50	4 0	...	6 30	7 30	9 32	9 26	9 35			
Dunstable, Church St.	7 10	8 40	9 45	11 5	12 48	2 0	4 10	...	6 40	7 42	9 38	9 35	9 45			
„ L. & N.W. arr.	7 15	8 45	9 50	11 10	12 53	2 5	4 15	...	6 45	7 50	9 45	9 40	9 50			
„ ....dep.	7 30	9 10	9 55	11 20	2 20	2 20	4 55	6 30	7 30	8 15	...	...	...			
LEIGHTON	7 45	9 25	10 10	11 35	2 35	2 35	5 10	6 45	7 45	8 30						

The ORIGINAL LOCAL LIST, PRINTED (gratuitously, for the accommodation of the Public)

Train times between Leighton and the Great Northern lines prior to the introduction of direct through running Dunstable with the new station of 1866.
S Summerson

The deep cutting of the climb of Sewell Bank up to Dunstable looking
towards Leighton Buzzard and Stanbridgeford
Stephen Summerson

Gateman instructions on other lines apart from the Dunstable branch.
Cyril Gibbins Collection

27

Working timetable (Down, Week Days Only) — Dunstable branch, 1921.

Station list (repeated for each section): LEIGHTON BUZZARD dep. — Grovebury Siding — Stanbridgeford — Gower's Siding — Forder's Siding — DUNSTABLE arr. — " L.N.W. dep. — "(Church St.) G.N. " — Chaul End Halt — LUTON, G.N. arr.

NOTE.—The Level Crossing Gates are closed against the Line each week night from after the passage of the 9.50 p.m. train Leighton till 6.50 a.m., and from after the passage of the 9.50 p.m. from Leighton, Saturdays, to 6.50 a.m., Mondays. Any train running over the Branch between these hours must stop for the Fireman or Goods Guard to open and close the Gates unless special arrangements have been made beforehand for the Gates to be open.

Working timetable for the Dunstable branch of 1921 when the line was at a peak for its goods traffic, all the important sidings are in place.
John Lowe Collection

DUNSTABLE BRANCH.

UP. WEEK DAYS ONLY.

Distance from Dunstable (Miles)	Station	78 G.N. Goods	79	80 G.N. Light Engine	81	82 G.N. Pass.	83 G.N. Pass.	84 Pass	85	86 G.N. Pass.	87	88 Pass	89 G.N. Pass.	90 G.N. Light Engine	91	92 G.N. Pass.	93	94	95 Mineral.	96	97 Goods	98 G.N. King & Brnx	99	100 Pass	101	102
		a.m.		MO a.m.		a.m.	a.m.	a.m.		a.m.		a.m.	a.m.	a.m.		a.m.			a.m.		a.m.	a.m.		a.m.		
	LUTON, G.N. .... dep	4 40		5 25		6 20				7 34		8 30				10 29					10 5			11 20		
	DUNSTABLE (Ch. St.) G.N. arr	5 25		5 40		6 31		6 50		7 45		8 40	9 6			10 40			11 20		11 0			11 31		
	L. N. W. arr					6 34				7 48		8 45	9 17	9 24		10 43			11 30		11 16			11 34		
	dep							7 0				8 48	9 20								X			11 38		
	Forder's Siding																				12 0	4 10				4 5
	Gower's Siding											8 58									12 30			11 48		4 52
	Stanbridgeford											9 6	9 21									4 20				4 57
	Groveberry Siding												9 24													
	LGHTON BUZZARD arr							7 10																11 56		

UP. WEEK DAYS ONLY.

Miles	Station	103 G.N. Pass.	104	105	106 Pass	107	108 Goods	109	110 G.N. Pass.	111	112 G.N. Goods	113 G.N. Pass.	114 Mineral.	115 Mineral.	116	117 Goods	118	119	120 G.N. Pass.	121	122 Pass	123 Goods	124 G.N. King & Brnx	125	126 G.N. Pass.	127	128 G.N. Goods
		p.m.			p.m.		p.m.		p.m.		p.m.	p.m.	SO	SO		p.m.			p.m.		p.m.	p.m.			p.m.		p.m.
	LUTON, G.N. .... dep	12 20							1 5		1 10	1 30				2 15			2 42						3 55		4 5
	DUNSTABLE (Ch. St.) G.N. arr	12 31			1 5		1 15		1 16			1 41							2 53		3 10				4 0		4 52
	L. N. W. arr	12 34							1 19		1 47	1 44							2 56			8 25			4 9		4 57
	dep				1 15		1 25														3 20						
	Forder's Siding												1 30	2 55									4 10				
	Gower's Siding												2 40	3 0							3 28		4 20				
	Stanbridgeford										6 0																
	Groveberry Siding																										
	LGHTON BUZZARD arr										6 15											8 40			4 9		

UP. WEEK DAYS ONLY.

Miles	Station	129 Mineral.	130 Goods	131	132	133	134 Mineral.	135	136 G.N. Pass.	137	138 Pass	139	140 G.N. Pass.	141	142 Goods	143	144	145 G.N. Pass.	146	147 Pass	148	149 Goods	150	151 G.N. Pass.	152 G.N. Goods	153 Engine and Break	154 G.N. Pass.
		S p.m.	S O p.m.		p.m.		S p.m.		p.m.		p.m.		p.m.		p.m.			p.m.		p.m.		p.m.		p.m.	p.m.	p.m.	p.m.
	LUTON, G.N. .... dep								5 38		6 0		6 30		7 0			7 16		7 55				8 30	10 18	10 20	10 20
	DUNSTABLE (Ch. St.) G.N. arr		5 15				5 45		5 44		6 15		6 41		7 20			7 18		8 9		8 25		8 41	10 18	10 31	10 31
	L. N. W. arr	4 46	5 35				5 55		5 47		6 24		6 44		7 30			7 19		8 13		8 40		8 44			10 34
	dep	4 55	5 45																			8 50					
	Forder's Siding																			8 23							10 30
	Gower's Siding																			8 31							
	Stanbridgeford																										
	Groveberry Siding																										11 15
	LGHTON BUZZARD arr																										

NOTE.—The Level Crossing Gates are closed against the Line each week night from after the passage of the 9.56 p.m. from Leighton till 6.50 a.m., and from after the passage of the 9.50 p.m. from Leighton, Saturdays, to 6.50 a.m., Mondays. Any train running over the Branch between these hours must stop for the Fireman or Goods Guard to open and close the Gates, unless special arrangements have been made beforehand for the Gates to be open.

Section L.—Loading of Goods, Mineral, &c., Trains.

Points.	Class 5.		Class 4.		Classes 1 & 2.		Maximum Number of Waggons authorised, including Break Van.	Remarks.
	Minerals, including Break Van.	Goods, including Break Van.	Minerals, including Break Van.	Goods, including Break Van.	Minerals, including 20-ton Break Van.	Goods, including Break Van.		
	Tons.	Tons.	Tons.	Tons.	Tons.	Tons.		
SOUTHERN DISTRICT—								
Dunstable Branch—								
Leighton and Stanbridgeford	450	450	525	500	...	...	60	
Stanbridgeford to Dunstable	100	100	165	160	...	...	20	
Dunstable to Stanbridgeford	300	300	375	350	...	...	50	

Important loading restrictions on the branch, note the crucial difference to loadings between Stanbridgeford and Dunstable.
John Lowe Collection

BLOCK TELEGRAPH STATIONS—*Continued.*

DUNSTABLE BRANCH.
No Regular Trains are run over this Branch on Sundays. 3-Wire Instruments.

Dis. tance. Mls. Yds.	BLOCK POSTS.		CLOSED FROM
... ...	Leighton Buzzard, No. 2 (North) ...	S	Daily—10.0 p.m. to 6.0 a.m. / Week-ends—10.0 p.m. Saturdays to 6.0 a.m. Mondays.
.. 383	,, ,, No. 1 (South) ...	S	
.. 1684	Grovebury Crossing	S	Daily—12.0 night to 5.30 a.m. / Week-ends—12.0 night Saturdays to 5.30 a.m. Mondays.
3 168	Stanbridgeford Station	S	Daily—11.30 p.m. to 6.0 a.m. / Week-ends—11.30 p.m. Saturdays to 6.0 a.m. Mondays.
.. 553	De Berenger & Gower's Siding ...	S	Opened only when required.
... 757	Forder's Siding	S	
1 1283	Dunstable Station	H	Daily—12.0 night to 5.0 a.m. / Week-ends—12.0 night Saturdays to 5.0 a.m. Mondays.

Wing, Ledburn, Billington, and Stanbridge Crossings open from 6.50 a.m. until the 9.50 p.m. Train from Leighton has passed.

Details of block telegraph.
John Lowe Collection

Collection and pick-up point for the TPO just south of Linslade Tunnel alongside the 'down' fast.
Colin Holmes Collection

The old road at Leighton Buzzard that crossed the railway over a level crossing until 1858. On the left is the Station Hotel building of that time. The entrance to the station was on the right behind the old building.
Bill Simpson

The bridge that carried the railway over the river and the Grand
Junction Canal. This was where the difficult short gradient caused
problems for long goods trains.
Bill Simpson

Linslade Tunnel at the north, the centre bore is from 1837, the left side
from 1859 with the new relief line that caused a move of the station. The
train is on the 1872-4 bore which is the 'down' fast. This is the narrowest
bore on the line and causes much turbulance at speed.
Bill Simpson

Linslade Tunnel of the original London & Birmingham Railway seen from the Linslade side.
National Railway Museum

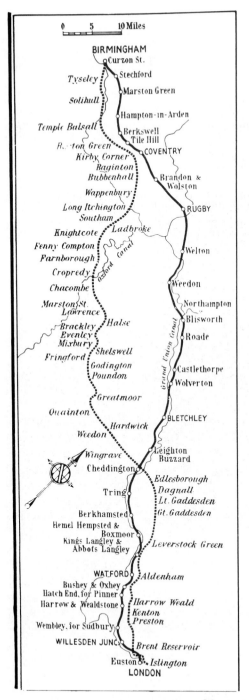

Leighton Buzzard came close to not being on the main line as this plan of 1824 by Sir John Rennie clearly shows (broken line). Powerful landed interests at the time made sure this plan did not succeed.
Railway Magazine

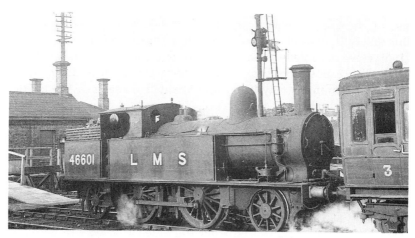

One of the 5ft 6in 2-4-2 tanks at Leighton Buzzard with the branch train on May 11, 1949.
H C Casserley

CHAPTER TWO

The London Midland & Scottish Railway

As a result of the Railway Act of 1921 the great amalgam of railways became empowered to take place from New Year's day January 1923 when the London Midland & Scottish Railway came into existence. This company now had control of over 40 percent of the total route mileage of England, Scotland and Wales with 19,000 track miles and 250,000 staff operating 7,500 engines. By the standards of 1923 an undreamt of monolith. It absorbed all the former undertakings of the LNWR and the whole was divided into three divisions, North, Midland and Western. The branch to Dunstable came under the Western Division control, a small but lucrative jewel. All the freight contracts on the line were at their peak and continued until the first blemish being the closure of Forder's Siding in 1938, the depressed thirties.

The LMS improved matters at Leighton by adding the 'fast' to 'slow' junction connection in 1927. This junction was to play a significant and tragic role at 12.21pm on a Sunday March 22, 1931 when the 11.30 am from Euston non stop to Crewe, hauled by one of the new 'Royal Scot' class 4-6-0's no 6114 'Coldstream Guardsman' passed over the junction from the down 'fast' to down 'slow' at excessive speed and was unable to remain on the track. The result was that the engine overturned and ploughed into the permanent way bringing with it five coaches. Six people were killed including the driver Hudson and fireman Rogers, both of Camden loco depot. The signalman of Leighton no 1 Thomas Troughton explained that the diversion was instructed because of engineering work on the 'fast' line. The only conclusion that could be drawn was that the driver was not aware of the temporary instruction. The signalman reported that it was evident that the driver had suddenly realised what was happening as the engine began to pitch and roll as he applied the brakes and sparks showered from the wheels. It was to no avail however as the locomotive lurched over on its side bringing coaches with it continuing in this way for some sixty yards. The derailment was across four tracks with only the rear bogie of the last coach remaining on the rails.

The one fortunate aspect of the catastrophe was that the first four coaches carried few passengers as two of them were the Kitchen Car and Restaurant Car. Neverthless in one of these vehicles there was a fatality, J Taylor aged twenty-one, a Dining Car cook. The Waiting Room at Leighton became a temporary mortuary. The others killed were Miss Dorothy Lang, Sir George Saltmarsh, Henry M Naftalin, Thomas Henry Hudson, Driver, Sidney Rogers, Fireman.

Later Sir Joseph Stamp President of the LMSR came to look at the wreckage as four steam cranes worked and by 10 o' clock that night the main line had been significantly cleared to allow two expresses, the night postal and the Irish Mail. The 9.6 am from Bletchley to Euston was able to run the following morning. This was a remarkable feat of work in view of the extent of the strewn wreckage.

After an inquest the following Tuesday, the bodies were returned to the families for burial. A melancholy duty for the down 'Royal Scot' was to make an unscheduled stop at Leighton to convey the body of Miss Dorothy Lang on to Glasgow.

Details from the inquest indicate that the speed restriction was set at 20 mph and the train had passed the Cheddington signalman Arthur Seyell at 60mph at 12.16 pm. At 12.19 pm he received the instruction from Leighton box 'obstruction danger'. The distance between the boxes was three miles one thousand yards, the usual time for an express over this distance was four to five minutes; this train had passed over it in just under four. Thomas Troughton at Leighton said:

'I first saw the train about half a mile from my box and I put my hand on the 'home' signal to lower it. I was alarmed to realise that there was not to be any reduction in speed. My first thought was to keep the train on the 'down' fast but by this time it was too near for me to do this. The train passed through the junction at a speed close to 55mph.' The 'home' signal is cleared when the train has reduced speed to the level of the limit.

Colonel A H Mount Inspecting Officer of railways presided over the Inquiry and had some criticism for the guard since it now appeared that the footplate crew were not informed of the speed restriction on 'Special Notices'. He recommended that the guard should ensure that he receives and signs for 'Special Notices'. The Officer went further in criticism of the Company stating that had Automatic Train Control been in operation in conjunction with the distant signal and with an audible warning the driver could not have ignored the restriction.

Another problem with this class of engine was the situation of smoke and steam obscuring the driver's vision. The point was raised by the Company who stated that experiments were taking place with various designs of baffle plates around the chimney. A few months later 'Coldstream Guardsman' had been repaired and brought back into service with smoke deflectors seen in November of the same year.

Further reinforcement of the issue of Automatic Train Control was brutally evident when on Friday October 13, 1939 the Euston - Stranraer express crashed with its 590 tons into the Euston - Inverness train at Bletchley station. The latter train was double-headed and again it was a case of a train going through opposing signals resulting in four fatalities and forty injured. The driver of the leading engine, Cyril Haynes faced a charge of manslaughter, driver Copperwheat on the train engine was also a driver of the 'Coronation Scot'. More men would have been killed but for the quick thinking of a member of Bletchley station staff who realised very quickly what was going to happen and shouted to all men to get clear; two were working in the van that took the immediate impact.

In July 1938 'Coronation' class 'Princess Alice' failed at Leighton Buzzard with the 'Coronation Scot' and was taken to Bletchley shed.

In 1947 the heaviest snowfall of the century which came in mid-February closed the Dunstable branch for several days.

Driver Fred Frazer recollects days at Leighton on the branch.

'I started at Bletchley in 1937 and was there for two years before being transferred to Leighton were I stayed until it was closed in 1962. When they closed it I had to go back to Bletchley as a redundant driver. I then learned diesels, especially railcars which I drove from Bletchley to Oxford, Banbury, Bedford and Cambridge; I even went through as far as Didcot with the diesels.

My first job at Leighton I was on the ash pits and coaling engines, a hard job from a wagon, I had to wait two years to become a fireman, and when I did I went onto the branch in 1939.

On the branch we always worked the engine forward towards Dunstable then came back to Leighton going tender first. I remember the trip two or three times a week with gas coal for Dunstable gas works. After the long drag to reach Dunstable the gradient dropped down into the station. We would have fourteen wagons of gas coal so we had a word with the signalman at Dunstable North saying that we wanted to 'trip' shunt them. We should have run round the train by rights, but we uncoupled the engine and ran forward to an adjoining siding leaving the train clear. The guard would then release the brake on the van and the train would run down under its own gravity into the Gas & Coke Siding, I used to jump onto the brake van as it went by.

During the war we had a good run with 'Churchill' battle tanks from Vauxhall's at Luton; they were a good test of skills on the gradient. They came down on special vehicles with vacuum fitted stock with guard's brake vans, one next to the engine then two tanks one in the middle of the train then two more tanks and another at the end of the train. These were brought down the line to Wing Sidings were they were assembled into long trains to be hauled away to the south coast. Each train would be hauling four tanks at ten miles an hour. We would stop and put all the brakes on at the top of the gradient. The engine would be the usual Super D, we had ten of these at Leighton just for working branch traffic. When we got to Gower's we would release all the brakes and carry on towards Leighton and Wing yard, where there were seven or eight sidings. Three trains would come down from Vauxhall's and back them into the sidings to make one train ready for departure, that would then be twelve tanks.

Also during the war we would help troop trains and ambulance trains over the 1 in 40. We would stand by at Stanbridgeford

Sidings and wait for the twelve bogies hauled by a Black Five to come from Leighton. He would pass by us onto the gradient and we would run up behind as he slowed down near Gower's. As he began to take the strain we would buffer up to him and start to push with the Super D. He soon slowed down when he hit that gradient but the old D would be in there and give him a good shove easily over the top. The Black Fives were good engines but their wheels were too big for that gradient, it was a real slog. It was from Stanbridgeford Siding that we picked up flowers from Wallace's of Eaton Bray, we used the normal passenger trains for this job picking up a van from the sidings. We brought it into Leighton, unhooked it from the motor train and ran round it, then we waited until the Northampton train was in and shunted the bogie van onto the back of it.

Our passenger working through to Luton was always with the push and pull, mostly with the Webb 'Coal Tank' or occasionally with a 2-4-2 tank. When occasionally the passenger engine broke down they would replace it with one coach hauled by one of the Super D's as of course this engine was not fitted for push-pull work.

During the depressed thirties some goods engines were displaced from the Lancashire & Yorkshire area and were sent south to Bletchley and Leighton. We called them 'Gracie Fields', on the branch they could manage ten wagons on the gradient which wasn't bad for a 3F compared to fourteen with a Super D which was 7F. There was certainly plenty for them to do as we were running seven sand trains and five chalk trains every day. Of course we would enjoy a bit of refreshment at the popular Tremarco's Cafe near Grovebury Crossing.

Our first train out in the morning was to Gower's with empties usually seventy wagons, we would leave a 5 o'clock in the morning. When we reached Stanbridgeford we ran round the wagons and pushed them into the sidings at Gower's. There was a little pointsman's lever box where you went in to operate the points for the siding. We then collected full wagons from the siding and took them back to Leighton Buzzard. On arriving back we then collected the empty sand wagons and went back up the branch to do the same thing with them at Grovebury

At Leighton we had ten Super D's and one 'Coal Tank' engine for the passenger trains. If any work needed doing fitters used to come from Bletchley to work on the engines and we did our own boiler washouts.

When they closed the branch we went to Bletchley but they still had some trains on the branch running after official closure. They ran under 'one engine in steam' restrictions where you had to close and open the crossing gates yourself. But that was only as far as Grovebury as these trains carried spoil for dumping from the rebuilding of Euston. We left the wagons on the siding and went back to Leighton light engine.

I remember after closure of the Aylesbury branch we did an errand down there on a Wednesday for cattle. We took the 'Coal Tank' picked up the cattle at Cheddington that had been left by a parcel train and went down the branch. We had to open and close the crossing gates ourselves. When we got to Broughton Crossing we couldn't find the Crossing lady to get the keys and unlock the gates, so I went round the back of the house and there she was sitting in the tin bath in the garden, she had the key by her and she simply handed it to me!'

The Vauxhall Motor factory at Luton made Churchill tanks from June 1941 onwards. Ten other companies made them besides Vauxhall. They first saw action during the Dieppe raid in August 1942 and were later used in North Africa and Italy.

The two road shed at Leighton Buzzard looking north with one of the former L&YR 0-6-0 ('Gracie Fields') locos evident no 12103. The probable time is circa 1930's when these engines were displaced from the north.
Ian Bowley Collection

'Warwells' of tanks being shunted by an army shunter, this is how the trains from Vauxhall's would have looked in Wing yard.
Bill Simpson Collection

LEIGHTON BUZZARD, DUNSTABLE, and LUTON.—(**Third class only**).

Miles	Week Days only.	mrn	mrn		aft	aft	aft	aft	aft
	463London (Euston) ..dep.	5 10	8 35	..	**S**	**E**	3F6	6 6	..
—	Leighton Buzzard.....dep.	7 36	1254	..	..	..	5 30	7 52	..
4½	Stanbridgeford	7 43	1 3	..	..	..	5 37	7 59	..
7½	**Dunstable** (L. M. S.) arr.	7 50	1 9	..	..	..	5 44	8 6	..
	dep.	7 55	..	..	1 27	1 50	6 21	..	8 30
8½	Dunstable Town...........	7 59	..	..	1 31	1 54	6 26	..	8 34
12½	**Luton** (L. N. E.) 854 .. arr.	8 8	..	..	1 40	2 3	6 35	..	8 44

Miles	Week Days only.	mrn		aft	aft	aft	
	Luton (L. N. E.) ....dep.	8 30	..	1245	5 46	7 32	..
4½	Dunstable Town............	8 40	..	1254	5 56	7 43	..
5½	**Dunstable** L. M. S.) arr.	8 43	..	1259	6 0	7 46	..
	dep.	8 45	..	1 16	6 10	8 15	..
8½	Stanbridgeford.. 412, 463	8 53	..	1 24	6 20	8 23	..
12½	**Leighton Buzzard**.... arr.	9 1	..	1 32	6 28	8 31	..
52½	**464London** (Euston) .. arr.	1140	..	3X13	9 0	1122	..

E Except Sats. F Dep. 3 20 aft on Sats. **S** Sats. only.
X 5 mins. later on Sats.
LOCAL TRAINS between Dunstable and Luton, 854

LONDON, CHEDDINGTON, and AYLESBURY.—(**Third class only**).

Miles	**Down.** Week Days only.	mrn		mrn	aft		aft	aft	aft
	463London (Euston)..dep.	5 10	..	8 35	12A15	..	415	6 6	715
—	Cheddington ....dep.	7 22	..	1030	2 15	..	540	7 50	850
2¾	Marston Gate......[1073a	7 32	..	1038	2 21	..	545	7 55	858
7	**Aylesbury 48, 830,** arr	7 45	..	1053	2 30	..	554	8 4	911

Miles	**Up.** Week Days only.	mrn	mrn		aft	aft	aft		aft
	Aylesbury ....dep.	6 40	8 5	..	1 5	4 50	6 35	..	8 15
4½	Marston Gate	6 49	8 14	..	1 15	4 59	6 44	..	8 24
7	**Cheddington 463.** arr.	6 55	8 20	..	1 21	5 5	6 50	..	8 30
43	**464London** (Eus.) arr.	8 18	9 41	..	3X13	7 2	9 0	..	..

A Dep. 12 50 aft. on Sats. X 5 mins. later on Sats.
OTHER TRAINS between London and Aylesbury, see pages 48, 830, and 1073

Wartime timetable for 1942 of the service between Leighton and Luton from Bradshaw's Guide.
Bill Simpson Collection

Leighton Buzzard
Observer report
tragic accident

The scene of the wrecked train at Leighton Buzzard station

'Coldstream Guardsman' having been re-railed at Leighton Buzzard showing the side of the locomotive that ran along the ground for some sixty yards on its side. Thus the buckled rail that has pierced the boiler lagging. The locomotive was back in service by the following November fitted with smoke deflectors.
Mrs T Pepper

One of a remarkable series of photographs of the wrecked train taken by a local photographer at Leighton Buzzard Mrs T Pepper, whose husband subsequently became station Foreman in the 1950's.
Mrs T Pepper

A view of the wreckage of the train looking north.
Mrs T Pepper

OPPOSITE PAGE: Four steam cranes were involved in moving the
wreckage, here one can be seen looking from the direction of the town.
Engines 9405, 9263 0-8-0's and 4157 0-6-0 were working at the site
removing smashed vehicles and debris.
Mrs T Pepper

Formerly of the LNWR, 0-8-0 goods engine no 49352 on an 'up' freight near Linslade tunnel on October 2, 1948.
Colin Stacey

'Royal Scot' class 6141 'The North Staffordshire Regiment' passing through Bletchley in May 1938 with an 'up' express, the entire class now fitted with smoke deflectors.
L Hanson

Evacuees at Leighton Buzzard station, there were two periods of
evacuation, the first in September 1939, then late 1940. It is not known
from which year this scene is taken, it is neverthless filled with the
poignancy of separation and bewilderment.
Colin Holmes Collection

Engine no 6917 an 18in (LNWR) Tank that was allotted a British
Railways number of 46917 then scrapped in April 1949. It is seen here on
the branch service on October 2, 1948.
B W L Brooksbank

The large express locomotive was the magnum opus of the LMS, here
46201 of the 'Princess Royal' class 'Princess Beatrice' is seen on
a 'down' train passing through Leighton Buzzard station in the early
fifties.
RAS

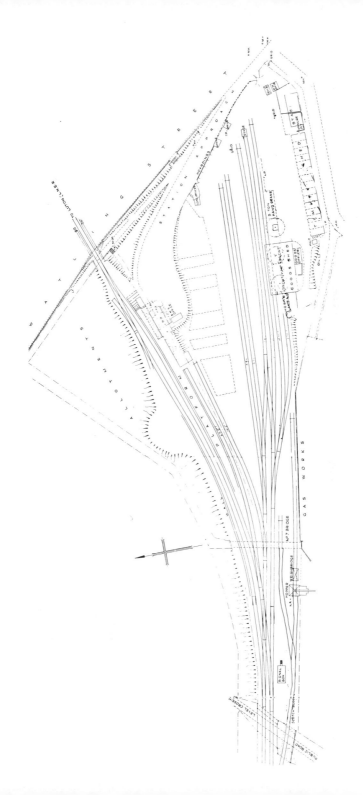

Dunstable station during the period of the LMS

LICHFIELD T.V. TO LONDON (EUSTON) AND BRANCHES

ADDITIONAL RUNNING LINES.	STATIONS AND SIGNAL BOXES, ETC.	Distance from place next above. Miles.	Yards.	UP LINE.	Lie-by Sidings and holding capacity. No. of Wagons. Down Side.	Up Side.	RUNAWAY CATCH POINTS. WHERE SITUATE.	LINE.	Approximate Gradient. 1 in	ENGINE WHISTLES. UP. Main, Fast or Passenger Line.	Slow or Goods Line.	DOWN. Main, Fast or Passenger Line.	Slow or Goods Line.	TO	SPEED RESTRICTIONS. MILES PER HOUR. UP.	DOWN.
							DUNSTABLE STATION TO LEIGHTON BUZZARD No. 2.									
	Dunstable—Station (Level Crossing)		—							1 short and 1 crow		1 short and 1 crow		Sidings and vice versa		
										1 long and 1 crow		1 long and 1 crow		To and from main platform		
														To and from bay		
														Crossover	45	45
	Stanbridgeford—Forder's Siding	1	1283												15	
							Between Dunstable and Leighton Buzzard, except as otherwise shown									
							From Dunstable to Stanbridgeford, descending Incline									
	„ De Berenger and Gower's Siding	—	757													
	„ Station (Level crossing)	—	653													
	Leighton Buzzard—Billington Level crossing	2	1116													
	„ Grovebury Crossing	—	712													
	„ Ledburn Level crossing	—	1034							1 and 1 crow		1 and 1 crow		Through		
	„ Wing Level crossing	—	268											Sidings and vice versa		
	„ No. 1 crossing	—	389											Crossover	35	35
	„ No. 2 (See page 62)	—	383													
							Between Wing level crossing and Leighton Buzzard station									
							AYLESBURY STATION TO CHEDDINGTON STATION.									
Staff & Ticket.	Aylesbury—Station (Level crossing)	—	—													
	Marston Gate—Station (Level crossing)	4	225													
	Cheddington—Mentmore Level crossing	2	65													
	„ Station (See page 63)	—	1145												45	45
							Between Aylesbury and Cheddington									

Section from the LMS Working Appendix for the branch in 1937.
Cyril Gibbins Collection

Dunstable North with a Craven class 105 diesel multiple unit no E51298 bound for Welwyn on August 5, 1963. To the right is a class 20 D8045 on the turntable road. In the far distance shunting the goods yard is 8 freight no 48755.
Southill Collection

CHAPTER THREE

British Railways

From midnight on December 31, 1947 the private ownership of Britain's railways ceased. What had been partially effected by two world wars was made an Act of Parliament and the railways went into public ownership, run by a Railway Executive under the British Transport Commission. The public name became British Railways.

What primarily concerned the Dunstable branch was that the entire route to Luton operated under one owner. The network was for operational reasons divided into regions with the branch being inside the London Midland Region (Western Division). Through trains continued to the Eastern Region to Welwyn and Hatfield and the motor train plied back and forth from Leighton Buzzard to Dunstable as before.

Much of the traffic continued as it had done under the LMS;

large tonnages of sand and chalk with the redoubtable former LNWR eight coupled engines showing remarkable ableness after so many years of this work.

Two years later on September 25, 1950 the original station at Dunstable was changed to Dunstable North the former GNR station Dunstable Church Street had become Dunstable Town on January 1, 1927. Nevertheless the locomotive shed closed November 5, 1962 and the staff were transferred to Bletchley.

The area came under the world spotlight on August 8, 1963 when the TPO mail was robbed of 2½ million pounds two miles south of Leighton station.

The transport system of the country was entering a period of fluidity and road freight traffic was increasing with the introduction of Motorways; the M6 in 1958 and the M1 in 1959. Industry was prepared to take advantage of government policy in this area and railway strikes had encouraged this since 1955. More personally the new family icon was to own one's own motor car and be liberated from the transport services altogether.

Sir Frank Markham who was MP for North Bucks was a champion of railways and fought hard in parliament against closure of the local rail services and the loss of mens' jobs. In 1962 the Newport Pagnell branch, Castlethorpe station and the Dunstable branch were marked up for closure. It was a difficult situation to defend. The 'Dunstable Dasher' was showing dwindling passenger returns from before the war when the little branch train had carried an average of 242 passengers on its first daily run to Dunstable. There were numerous excursions to the seaside from the branch and something of a highlight of the week would be the full trains on Saturday for spectators going to watch Luton Town football team play. By the 1950's buses were running between the towns and these seriously affected passenger receipts with a half-hourly timetable available, also increased ownership of the private car. Closure came for the passenger service on the section between Leighton Buzzard and Dunstable on June 30, 1962, as the last operating day, actual closure day being July 2, 1962. When driver Harry Crossley and fireman T Daniels drove the final train, along with guard Percy Dimmock, at 5.38pm. with at least three hundred passengers.

The station of Dunstable Town closed to passengers April 26, 1965 but had closed earlier to goods on December 7, 1964. The original Dunstable station closed to passengers April 26, 1965 but some goods traffic remained until October 9, 1967, for the service to Hatfield. Freight at Leighton Buzzard ceased on February 6, 1967 (Wing Road yard).

Heavy Chalk trains had continued to go over the branch after the passenger service had ceased, until it was crushed and mixed with water and pumped along a pipline. Arnold's Sands traffic gradually dwindled and returned to the road transport.

The tipping of spoil at Grovebury from the construction of the new Euston station kept the line open for a while. The track was finally pulled up in 1969. By 1971 there was a car park where the locomotive shed had been.

Before closure the very last working on the Leighton Buzzard - Dunstable branch December 5, 1969 was when Class 47 'Colossus' arrived at Arnold's Billington Sidings to remove a container wagon which had been used to deliver a container to the LBNGR purchased from Wolverton works.

Recollections of driver Maurice Conquest;

'I started at Leighton on January 16, 1942, when that closed I went on to Bletchley from where I retired in 1989.

You certainly had plenty to think about on that branch to Dunstable, what stands out in my mind were those chalk trains from Totternhoe often 40 wagons, the tricky part was working that train over the short rise over the Grand Union Canal then dropping before the 1 in 80 rise into Leighton where you were on a tight curve as well. We had to try to keep the couplings taught as we went down one gradient and rose up on the other, the guard for his part would try to hold them from going slack on the downward section so that there would be no snatch. When the train was approaching this section there would be a brakesman from the Carriage & Wagon Department at the side of the track ready to pin down the wagon brakes. The trouble was that even with their best efforts things would go awry. There were some couplings that we didn't realise were worn and flawed with age and if we were unfortunate to get a 'snatch' on one of these then there would be a 'breakaway'. You knew on the engine when they went and you had lost some, I have known some run back as far as Grovebury Crossing. When that happened the guard would whistle as loud as he could to let the crossing keeper know that there was a 'breakaway' and open the gates, it happened quite a few times. The best hope for stopping them was that you had managed to pin the wagon brakes down before they ran away, that could slow them.

Most were held in Wing yard when we got into Leighton but one working went straight onto the main line and headed north for Bilton (Rugby). This train would then return with fifty or so empties back for Totternhoe.

At 5.30 every night we had to leave tender first to Northampton with seventy wagons of sand. We had to go tender first as all our engines were boiler first for going to Dunstable on account of the 1 in 40 gradient, it could be difficult for the water level to run tender first up Sewell Bank. We had problems with no turntable, they had a turntable at Dunstable but there was not sufficient space to turn a Super D on it. One early morning coal train for Dunstable from Leighton was a particularly heavy load for the bank of twenty six wagons so we would go double heading to Stanbridgeford, stop in the station and unhook the front engine. He would then run forward and shunt back onto the 'up' line, we would then pass him and he would run up behind us when we had cleared the points, he didn't couple-up just ran up to us and pushed us.

We had plenty of cattle for Bunkers at Stanbridgeford. Stanbridgeford used to win a shield for the most revenue for an intermediate station, they had coal, cattle, flowers and the Totternhoe chalk works all on the accounting of a small country station.

Deliveries into Ledburn Wharf were all coal, it had two sidings. When you had wagons for Ledburn you would take them down the branch, leave them at Grovebury go on with the train then pick them up on the way back as you could only shunt Ledburn from the 'up' side. The coal merchants at Ledburn were Labrums, Franklin, Sproat, Bambrook and the Co-op.

The building at the back of the steam shed at Leighton was a herbalist factory with a short siding into it called Alder's Siding. When this became defunct c1957 we were quite pleased at Leighton shed because we had an awful dark dingy mess room inside the shed. This was replaced by a coach being placed on this siding for our use and offices for the shed foreman, it was quite an improvement I can tell you.

On the day of the 'blowback'* by 41222 I was at Dunstable I was in the yard on the usual Super D getting some clinker out of the fire. I hear the sound of this train approaching and I thought that he was going a bit fast for the station. I puts my iron down and had a look over the side and this train came into view doing about

* The 'blowback' on 41222 took place at 8.40 am April 20, 1955 between Chaul End Crossing and Dunstable Town station. The train crew were forced to jump from the engine and sadly the fireman lost his life as a result; the driver recovered from his injuries.

forty five mile an hour straight through the station. The gates were obviously set for the road and there were school children walking on both sides of the road by the gates going to school. The train came on at this speed and smashed through the gates and with what must have been providential mercy he didn't hit a single child. It then continued reaching the top of the 1 in 40 bank but providence had reached even further, as the damaged gates had caught the vacuum pipe and severed it so the brakes were on at the top of the bank. Had this not happened it would have continued on, the injectors were still on and there was 48psi still in the boiler. The actual 'blowback' had occurred on the section between Dunstable and Luton at the place called 'Skimpot'. I was the first person on the engine after it came to a stand, the footplate was ominously empty, I looked at the firehole doors where all that flame had come through a gap of about four inches. There was a spare headlamp on a bracket and this had been completely melted and a nearby brush was just pure cinder. Then Charlie and I managed to repair the vacuum and set back into the platform and worked that train and passengers on to Leighton. Had she gone down that bank she would certainly have come off with a two coach train of passengers. Both driver and fireman had jumped from the engine immediately as the 'blowback' occurred.

When we went off to Bilton with the chalk at 3.00 am Monday morning we would often be pulling fifty-seven wagons from the sidings at Leighton and they had been standing all weekend on grease axle boxes. If we had had a heavy frost over the weekend it used to make it very difficult to move them as the boxes were all stiff, we often used two engines to get it out of the loop, one would stay with us to no 2 signalbox then hook off. Once we got going we would be put on the 'down' fast which would mean the small bore tunnel at Linslade, that was real murder, luckily it wasn't any longer as the exhaust would shower us on the footplate as there was barely any space around the train, we would be as low as we could get gasping for breath. We had to put plenty of coal on to get steam and years ago we used to have ballast trains with men going along picking up coal that had been dislodged from engines going through by the close proximity of the blast. When the express passenger train approached the tunnel at sixty or seventy the drivers would pull their coats over their heads to protect themselves from the dust that would circle the interior of the cab at high speed caused by the enormous turbulence of hitting the small bore tunnel at high speed.

Leighton shed had fourteen sets of men arranged in two 'links'. Main line 'link' for working Northampton, Tring, Swanbourne, Verney Junction, with a separate branch working 'link'. A foreman and three labourers were also based here.'

Bert Smith guard started on the railway in 1949 in Alloa. He came to Leighton Buzzard in February 1953 returning to his childhood area.

'At that time we had an average of a about sixty to seventy wagons a day from Arnold's and Garside's sand pits. Also four to five trains a day from Totternhoe of chalk for the Rugby Portland Cement with up to forty-two twenty seven ton wagons in a train. The chalk traffic was eventually lost because they decided to crush it and mix it with water and send it along a pipeline to Rugby, that was about 1964-65 time.

The way that I tackled the tricky rise over the canal then rising to 1 in 80 into the station was that as I came through Billington Crossing I warmed the 'blocks' up, that is to say I put the brakes on a bit. Because my brake van was only twenty tons and I would be in charge of a thousand ton train and by doing that I could ease the brake on without snatching and keep the couplings fairly tight all the time. An interesting example was with the 5.30am from Gowers, one morning as we reached Black Bridge I had the blocks on tight then suddenly I had a breakaway with seven and as I looked back I could see that Wing gates had started to close. Luckily he saw what had happened and he opened them quickly. So I let them roll and brought them to a stand eventually at just short of Ledburn, so I had stopped them between the crossings.

With Sewell Bank if on going up the train came to a standstill with the regulation of fourteen 16-ton wagons wagons the procedure was to put the brake van hard on and unhook seven. He would then continue to Dunstable yard with the front end of the train then reverse back to pick up the remaining. Most drivers did get stuck at some time, the only one that never got stuck was Ernie Bryant he used to get his fireman to walk ahead of the slow moving train with a watering can full of sand which he used to trickle on the track in front of the uncoming train, he never got stuck.

On the chalk trains we had about thirty 16-ton wooden bodied wagons, then in about 1955 it was increased to a maximum of 42 twenty-seven ton capacity 'chalk tippler' steel bodied wagons hauled by 'Super D' 0-8-0's with a 20-ton brake at the back.

Sometimes if I had a lot of coal dust in the van I would wait until the train was under way at speed then open my back door and front together and that would sweep out all the coal dust in one moment, especially when Sandy Dewhurst was your driver. We once left Leighton with a load for Northampton of sixty wagons of sand and at Wolverton we passed an express train with the locomotive at the head called 'Barham'. I remember looking up to see this driver with his hand on the regulator looking at us in complete disbelief as we passed by him with a 'Super D' 0-8-0 goods engine. And when we got to Northampton I had a word with his fireman who said, 'I'm bloody knackered Bert, as fast as I was putting it in the fire he was blowing it out the chimney!'.

Linslade Tunnel 'down' fast was an interesting situation, before you got there you had to make sure that you put all of your gear on the inside, the lean of the brake with the track elevation was so severe that everything would go flying across if you did not do that.

When Vauxhall had a £30 million pound extension we had some good loads up Sewell Bank then, all the girders were taken and stored in the yard at Dunstable. It was in about 1958 time and with these bogie bolsters we could only take three up the bank at once. Then cranes came along and loaded them onto lorries in Dunstable yard.'

The passenger's view of the train reversing into Stanbridgeford siding to collect flowers and fruit in fitted vans
B K B Green

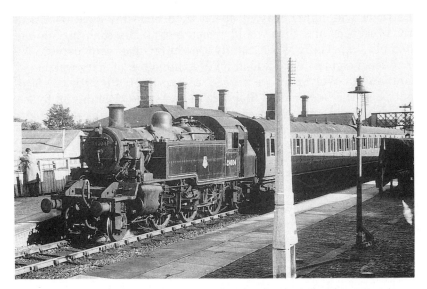

One of the light 2-6-2 Standard tanks that occasionally did branch line
duty along with the Ivatt engines. This is number 84004 waiting at the
branch platform on June 8, 1957.
H C Casserley

Interior of Wing Crossing box with Arthur Pepper Leighton Buzzard
station foreman acting as relief signalman about to close gates
Mrs T Pepper

'Jubilee' 4-6-0 'Rodney' held at the 'down' slow platform as the driver fixes a studied gaze on the photographer. Beyond the train is the station goods shed on the site of the original station.
Mrs T Pepper

Leighton Buzzard station looking south on May 25, 1962. A Standard class 5MT has been brought to a halt on the 'down' slow.
Peter E Baughan

A mixed freight on the 'up' slow hauled by one of the legendary
Black 5 4-6-0's no 44762
Mrs T Pepper

Stanbridge Mead Crossing and keeper's house between Stanbridgeford
and Grovebury. The signalman's hut on the right contained only a
couple of repeater instruments.
Kevin Lane

Maurice Conquest who describes working the branch elsewhere in this book looks down from 46601 a regular branch engine in the late forties.
Maurice Conquest

Ledburn Crossing where class 25 brings mineral empties to be shunted. The gates are being manually operated by the train crew, the guard Bert Smith who submitted contribution to this book can be seen standing by the gates.
Ian Bowley

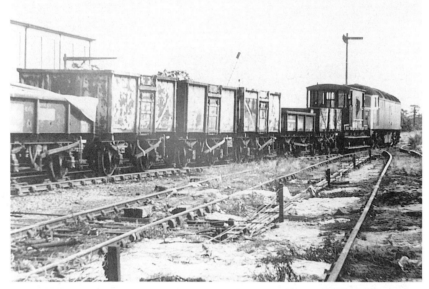

Class 47 shunting wagons of sand and swarf at Grovebury sidings near the tipping dock in the early sixties. Note how the modern diesel compares with the former LNWR lower quadrant signal of the 'up' line home at the crossing. The building behind the train is that of H W Gossard. Guard Bert Smith described how dangerous it was shunting in the dark here as there were no lights after Gossard's switched them out after 6 o'clock. All that he had then was a feeble oil lamp to try to see all the wires and equipment that could so easily trip a person alongside moving wagons.
Ian Bowley

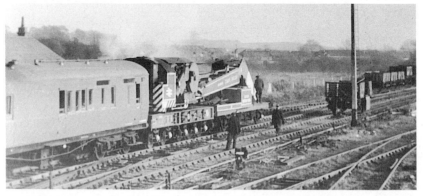

A steam crane recovers wagons from the sand tipping dock in the early sixties.
Ian Bowley

Although it is not clearly visible the demolition train is in the distance at the foot of Sewell Bank. As members of the Iron Horse Society prepare to rescue Gower's Siding signalbox which was 553 yards on the Dunstable side of Stanbridgeford station. Still visible is the trailing connection from 'down' line to 'up' for the siding. Members seen here removing the box on January 19, 1969 are from left to right Chris Daniels and Robin Wilson. They paid Thomas Ward the demolition contractor £7.10 shillings (£7.50) for the cabin and its equipment. The signalling equipment was used on the LBNGR but the 8ft square cabin did not survive deterioration.

Dunstable branch Working timetable for the period January 4 to June 13 1965 weekdays only

Station					6.15 ex Southam		Engine & Brake		LE		
Leighton Buzzard dep	5.35	6.0	7.22	9.0	9.37	10.30	11.40	12.15	2.30	4.40	4.15
Grovebury Siding			7.30								
Gower's Siding	5.55			9.18	9.55		11.55	12.45	2.45		4.15
Dunstable North arr	6.25				10.55					4.50	

Station												
Dunstable North dep			9.20				12.25					6.15
Gower's Siding	6.25			10.10	10.45			1.15		4.00	5.50	
Grovebury Siding		8.30				11.12						
Ledburn			9.40									
Leighton Buzzard arr	6.35	8.40	10.05	10.25	11.00 to Southam	11.22	12.45	1.30	3.45	4.35	6.00	6.35

Note: The last chalk train ran from Totternhoe (Gower's Siding) to Southam on April 15 1965. The Working timetable for June 14, 1965 to April 17 1966 shows only two 'Q' trains from Grovebury Siding to Leighton Buzzard

Detailed notes of the final working time table on the branch.
Stephen Summerson

Grovebury Crossing in the mid sixties with sand and fertiliser wagons looking towards Leighton Buzzard. The type 4 signalbox of the LNWR is still in use in the last days of its long lifespan.
Ian Bowley

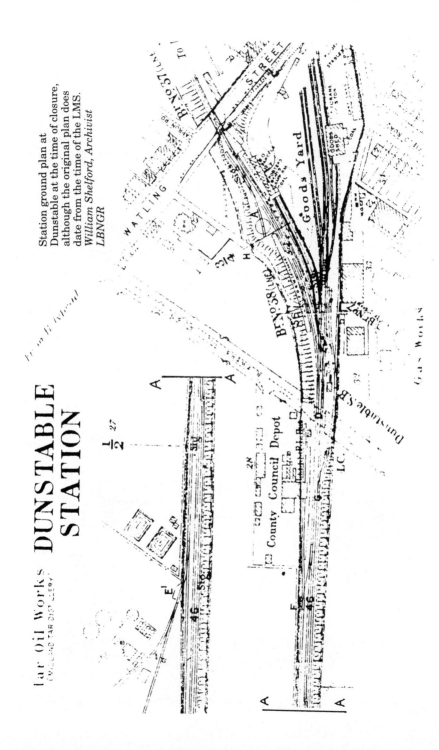

Station ground plan at Dunstable at the time of closure, although the original plan does date from the time of the LMS. *William Shelford, Archivist LBNGR*

The final day of the 'Dunstable Dasher' as it takes centre stage at
Leighton Buzzard with driver Harry Crossley and fireman T Daniels.
F Parkinson

Special train 'The Banburian' at Dunstable, June 1962.
F Parkinson

The long goodbyes as the last scheduled passenger train leaves
Stanbridgeford on June 30, 1962
F Parkinson

Sand 'Dobbers' quarrying the sand at Leighton Buzzard using horse drawn railway tipper wagons.
Bill Simpson

CHAPTER FOUR

The Leighton Buzzard Narrow Gauge Railway

It is fortunate that the tireless energies of a few preservationists turned their attentions to the district as the railway life of the area was coming to a close in the 1960's. We as inheritors of all the meaningful history of the industrial life of this nation are indebted to their efforts.

There have been excavations from sand quarries in the district since 1850 around Grovebury when sand was taken by Grand Junction canal from Linslade destined for the glass works at West Bromwich. In 1899 there was a proposal for a Leighton Buzzard and Hitchin Light Railway to connect with the burgeoning sand developments, but this came to nothing. Even though the sand is of fine quality, from fine silica sand for glass making to foundry sand, it remained a small scale industry. What competed against it was the cheap Belgian sand that came to this country in the form of ballast in ships. With the outbreak of the war in 1914 this supply was immediately affected and great demand was made to the Leighton Buzzard district which had only a rudimentary road transport system available to convey very heavy requirements. What we now call the road infrastructure was severely damaged by this traffic. During the

69

war traction engines, steam lorries and horses were used to haul the sand to the railway which had a severe effect on the roads. Maintenance of them was subsidised by the government at £1,000 per month as it was classified as war material. When the war ended the quarrying system had become much more developed and financially successful, it could not return to the bucolic horse and cart of former years, it needed to have a rail network to keep it viable. The two main sand companies at Leighton Buzzard being Joseph Arnold and George Garside.

The plans for this industrial railway of 2ft gauge extended 4½ miles were laid before Leighton Buzzard UDC at a meeting on April 17, 1919. These plans were viewed with sufficient support for a further meeting to be held at the Swan Hotel, Leighton Buzzard on June 3, 1919. This was chaired by J H Green and supported by A and E Arnold, sons of Joseph Arnold, H Delafield, R G Walton, A W Berry and H W Clough. It was supported also by Mr George Garside who could not be present. Almost all of the required capital was subscribed from this meeting with the sand merchants contributing one third of the whole. They were able to guarantee for ten years a minimum annual traffic of 70,000 cubic yards bringing an expected return on capital of 10% per annum.

As a result the company of Joseph Arnold & Sons Limited and George Garside (Sand) Limited largely established the Leighton Buzzard Light Railway Limited that was incorporated on July 26, 1919 to build a railway system to carry sand from the workings to the railhead at Grovebury Sidings on the Dunstable branch of the then LNWR. The line was to run from Double Arches to the railway sidings alongside Billington Road. It was an independent company with a nominal capital of £20,000 issuing 20,000 shares at £1 each, estimated capital expenditure to bring the railway to operation was estimated at £15,000. There was little time to waste and the work began as soon as it could in building the 3¼ miles of railway and the grand opening took place on November 20, 1919. However haste had overcome efficiency and the line was a problem. Rails were 28lbs per yard and gradients abounded with 1 in 25, 1 in 27 and 1 in 50. The nature of the construction can be appreciated when it is understood that no curved rails were used and curves were 'created' by bending straight track into the chairs. Nevertheless from that time on until 1969 sand was carried in enormous tonnages; 100,000 tons per annum in prosperous years, along the narrow gauge and onto the national system. At Arnold's Billington Road siding the sand was tipped from an 'L' shaped double track gantry into standard gauge wagons, one of several gantries in the Grovebury area. The LBLR had their locomotive and wagon repair building close to Billington Road Crossing.

The sand railway was at first worked by two Hudswell Clarke 0-6-0 well tank engines (nos 1377/78) which were purchased and converted from 60cm gauge. They were G class steam locomotives built in 1918 for the WD light railways and numbered 3207 and 3208, as they were never delivered to the WD they were bought from the makers. They were converted to 2ft gauge and sold to the LBLR for £1,000 each. Thought to be ideal the steam locomotives however did not prove popular on the railway, being regarded as being too 'smokey'. They suffered from the indifferent track laying, becoming often derailed, and were an inconvenience regularly needing water. They also got sand in the motion and were in all probability regarded as being too labour intensive in this very busy production environment that was much more easily catered for by petrol engine locos. They were dispatched from the system by 1922.

Another locomotive used in 1919 was a tractor type in two sizes, 20 and 40hp of two to six tons in weight built by Motor Rail Limited of Bedford which was given the name 'Simplex'. These had seen use in France during the war and proved ideal for this system and seven were bought and used on the LBLR but others were used in the adjacent quarries. One armoured type locomotive obtained from the War Department ran until 1955, also a petrol locomotive called 'Festoon'. These machines worked at the quarries for forty years until 1950 when they began to be replaced by more modern machines. In that year a new 2 1/2 ton 'Simplex' was delivered. In 1951 and 1954 two six ton locos of 40hp were also delivered, three of five tons followed in 1955 also 40hp. This brought the stock of engines up to six modern locomotives. At this time it was decided to reorganise the way that the LBLR worked and the new locos were taken over by the quarry owners, Arnold's and Garside's who then became responsible for handling their own trains and paid a toll to the railway.

The LBLR owned twenty-one locomotives but others were owned by the quarries where they worked and would often take a trip out on the 'main line'; these being the 20hp type. Quarry company locos worked in the quarries taking the skips of sand from the face, replacing the job of horses in the early days, to the washing plants or main line. The LBLR locos would then take the skips along the main line to the depots or to the standard gauge exchange sidings of Arnold's or Garside's accessed by open level crossings (three sited across the Billington Road).

Garside also had a separate system at Grovebury south of the Dunstable branch west of Grovebury Road level crossing and also the Leighton Buzzard Tile Works.

Some decline was precipitated by the rail strike of 1955 when quarry owners were forced to look to road alternatives which had improved considerably since the difficult days of 1919. On January 1, 1963 Arnold's became the sole owners of the LBLR.

In early 1969 British Rail gave notice of its intention to close the Dunstable branch which they did in December. With closure of the branch the traffic that remained was at the northern end of the line from Chamberlain's Barn Quarry and Stonehenge Brick Works. These were the twilight days of the entire operation, the final quarry was Munday's Hill Quarry where the last rail operation by Arnold's ceased in May 1981 when dumper trucks took over what transportation was required to load lorries.

In 1967 The Iron Horse Preservation Society was formed from narrow gauge enthusiasts led by Brian Harris and Laurie Brooks, they gained permission to operate steam hauled trains on the defunct section of which they rented two miles. This was at the south end where trains had now ceased as the branch was about to be lifted. They established their headquarters in an engine shed built by members adjacent to Pages Park near Billington Road sidings and the locomotive and wagon repair shop building of the former companies.

To run their railway the IHPS obtained four Simplex diesels, (two were cannibalised) from St Albans sand and gravel pits. Wagons came from the Colne Valley Water Board. The first passenger train ran on March 3, 1968 and in the summer months more than 3,000 visitors were carried on the little railway from Pages Park.

Later the name of the line was changed to Leighton Buzzard Narrow Gauge Railway Society. In 1970 two bogie wagons were converted from 1914-18 drop-sided wagons to covered coaches for the start of the running season at Pages Park. Also in 1970 engine 'P C Allen' was delivered after its owner Sir Peter Allen agreed to loan it through the Transport Trust. On July 24, 1970 two Simplex diesels were donated to the the LBNGR Society by Redland Flettons Limited from their Elstow works. About this time lease of some old stable buildings on the railway between

72

Vandyke Junction and Double Arches was negotiated. These were intended as a workshop and headquarters.

Against great odds railway restorers have proved determined people enduring all hardships and difficulties to retain the delight of a railway experience as much for others as themselves. The workers of the LBNGR are no exception, theirs was an industrial line not built or equipped to carry passengers, for it to do so meant years of continuous effort. It is a fitting tribute to those efforts that the line prospers and gives great pleasure to all those that care to visit it, which is well worth doing. Travelling the line today the pleasure is doubly enriched by knowledge of its history. It began as a roughly built industrial railway amongst sand workings where many men toiled for long hours in hard conditions. Now a steam hauled journey on a safe and robust permanent way will give the traveller cause for a pleasant reverie, an experience happily removed from the stresses of modern working lives.

'Dobbers' with horse drawn sand tipping wagon in the early years. *Colin Holmes Collection*

The diesel engine locomotives that worked the sand railway can still be
seen at Stonehenge Works on the LBNGR
Bill Simpson / LBNGR

One of the locos no 13 'Arkle' built in 1937 by Motor Rail Ltd 'Simplex'
Elstow Road, Bedford carried an unusual curved roof. This was one of
the last engines in use being withdrawn in 1982, formerly of George
Garside & Sons Ltd. it weighed 2.5 tons.
Bill Simpson / LBNGR

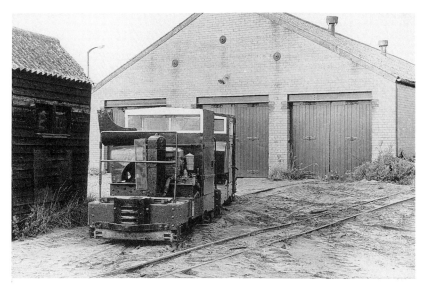

Reconditioned Motor Rail locos outside Arnold's workshops at
Billington road on September 30, 1976.
Kevin Lane

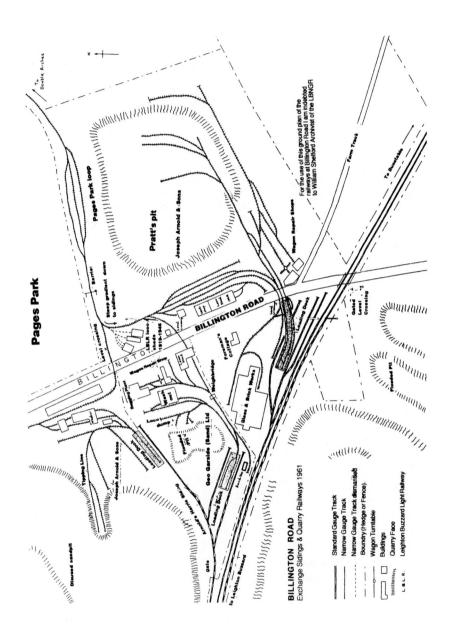

Pages Park

To Double Arches

Pages Park loop

Pratt's pit

Joseph Arnold & Sons

Barrie!

Steep gradient down to sidings

Level crossing

BILLINGTON ROAD

BILLINGTON ROAD

Level crossing

L.B.L.R. loco shed 1919/1945

Wagon Repair Shops

Loading Dock

Gated Level Crossing

Farm Track

To Dunstable

For the use of this ground plan of the railways at Billington Road I am indebted to William Shelford Archivist of the LBNGR

Foreman's Cottage

Weighbridge

Wagon Repair Shop

Tipping Point

Loco Loading dump

Joseph Arnold & Sons

Geo Garside (Sand) Ltd

Glass & Brick Works

Flooded Pit

Tipping Line

Joseph Arnold & Sons

Doulton tunnel

Arnold's loco shed

Loading Dock

Gate

To Leighton Buzzard

Disused sandpit

BILLINGTON ROAD
Exchange Sidings & Quarry Railways 1961

Standard Gauge Track
Narrow Gauge Track
Narrow Gauge Track dismantled
Boundry (Hedge or Fence).
Wagon Turntable
Buildings
Quarry Face
L.B.L.R. Leighton Buzzard Light Railway

76

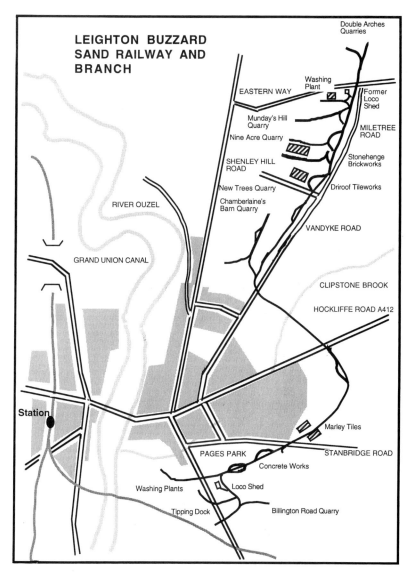

Ground plan of the track layout of the narrow gauge industrial railway that worked the district.

OPPOSITE PAGE: Ground plan of the connections with the standard gauge branch and the narrow gauge of the Leighton Buzzard Light Railway at Billington Road.
William Shelford, LBNGR

Alongside the loading dock at Arnold's Billington sidings Iron Horse members M Bowley and C Daniels unload spent ballast into the sand hopper wagons in May 1968.
Ian Bowley

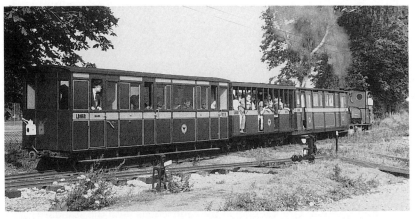

Pleasures of riding the narrow gauge, the public enjoying the experience of this once industrial line.
Bill Simpson

Arnold's Double Arches Quarry (North Pit) engine no 36 awaits
loading.
Kevin Lane

Garside's Munday Hill Quarry engine no 17 'Damredub' departs with
tipper wagons of sand.
Kevin Lane

Garside's train with no 29 'Ayala' leaving Double Arches crossing
Eastern Way with sand from Churchways Quarry for washing etc at
Eastern Way washing plant in May 1977.
Kevin Lane

LBLR c1930 with 20hp Motor Rail shunting Arnold's branch.
Ian Bowley Collection

Early this century the approach to Leighton Buzzard station
with milk carts and carrier carts assembled.
Shelia Turney

CHAPTER FIVE

Leighton Buzzard

Leighton station opened on April 9, 1838. This station had only
two facing platforms and almost inevitably, an 'up' goods ran
into a branch train waiting in the station in November 1857. The
result of this was that the Board of Trade insisted that the LNWR
construct a separate platform for the branch trains.

This demand coincided with greater events in the development
of the main line. Since 1838 many extended lines ran from the L
&B route; branches to Aylesbury, Bedford, Oxford and Banbury
and an important connection with the North Midland Railway to
Derby and York from Rugby. The railway was under intolerable
pressure with just the two sets of rails. It was therefore decided to
build an 'up' goods relief line from Bletchley to Primrose Hill
and this would affect the site of Leighton station. The new line
ran over the ground of the town side platform and required the

crossing to be closed and new diversionary roads to be built. The old original station was closed for passengers on February 14, 1859, and the new Leighton Buzzard station opened February 14, 1859. This was further rebuilt with the addition of the fourth loop line in 1874. With the introduction of this extra pair of tracks the station was developing much more and the signalling becoming much more complicated. As a result of this, control of the station was divided between two signalboxes 446 yards apart Leighton South and Leighton North in the 1877-78 period. One box was actually situated adjoining a platform but was moved with signalling developments after 1880. The boxes seen on the station plan in this book appear from plan view to be of the Saxby & Farmer type that were gradually replaced by LNWR standard types over the system.

When the London & Birmingham line was built there was opposition from vested interests of the Grand Junction Canal and local landowners who managed to have the route pass through Linslade rather than closer to the town. With the siting of the new station the railway company were still obliged to maintain the direct right of way along the old Aylesbury Road even though they had made alternative road construction of Springfield Road and widening of the Soulbury Road bridge. They were also required to build a footbridge, this was increased in the length and can be discerned as being in two sections.

The station building seen in the photograph in this book with two wings on each side of the entrance was completed in 1860. Further rebuilding was undertaken from 1956 to 1990. Originally the station was called simply 'Leighton', Buzzard being added in 1911.

The west portal of Linslade tunnel was added with the additional loop line in 1874. In 1956 improvements to the Dunstable side of the station buildings began and platform buildings were replaced at the station and new concrete awnings over platforms 4 and 6 were erected. The front entrance to the station was closed and the booking hall was moved to the side. Chimneys were removed from the station buildings and the brickwork was cleaned. In 1966 the main line was opened to electric traction.

In 1848 Leighton Buzzard had 971 tons of coal delivered which would have course been in the station area of the first station which appears to have had some yard facilities on the 'down' side. There must also have been some kind of siding to put the wagons clear of the running lines. Eventually the later station site had two goods depots and extensive siding facilities. North of the station on the 'up' side was a goods shed and sidings facilities for general merchandise and livestock but was so restricted that another goods shed had to be built at Grovebury with coal drops. Like the Loco steam shed this was a very confined site. Goods facilities at the station closed down in 1962 at Old Road.

As part of the developments of 1874 land was purchased south of the station alongside the branch to Dunstable to build sidings and goods facilities there. This came to be known as Wing Yard, and gave the station greater space to accumulate traffic that was developing with demand in the area. Road access to this yard was over Wing Crossing. This yard played such an important role in the intense build up of traffic from the sand and chalk workings and also the heavy wartime goods work. With post war decline the yard remained operational until February 6, 1967 when it closed down and what goods traffic remained was then handled by Grovebury area sidings. There was some consideration given to electrifying the branch up to these sidings during the electrification of the west coast main line in the 1960's. This was not done however and this final section of the Dunstable branch was closed from December 8, 1969.

Amongst the private sidings of the station area was a short siding of just a few yards alongside the steam shed with a loading dock into the yard of Robert Alder's medicinal manufacturers works. It only had one wagon length platform and fell into disuse in the early 1950's. This was seen as some relief by the steam shed staff who had their request for a mess coach granted by the Oerlikon Coach (ex-LNWR) being placed on this siding.

Grovebury Sidings to Dunstable (North) route was closed temporarily to through traffic on January 10, 1966; this was made permanent closure on June 12, 1967. Before total closure of the branch, with one engine in steam using both 'up' and 'down' lines, an important connection was put in at Luton on January 1, 1966 between Midland Road and Bute Street stations.

The first 'Commuter Express' was introduced in 1981. In 1989 the platforms were lengthened to accommodate twelve coach trains. And by September 1989, a £1.8 million project had begun to completely rebuild the station which was undertaken by Laing Construction Ltd of Luton and British Rail's own Civil Engineering department. It is a good indication of the importance of this branch to realise that there had been six private sidings between Billington Road level crossing and Grovebury Road crossing. Ledburn Wharf Siding (located by Ledburn Crossing) was used until the mid-1960's with road access from the Mentmore Road. This was a public siding handling domestic coal for several local merchants. The site of the siding is now occupied by the Mentmore Gardens housing development.

Sidings affected by closure were, Arnolds Billington siding; Garside's Billington Road siding; Garside's Rackley Siding on the south side of the line close to Grovebury Crossing signal box. This closed when Garside rationalised their operations and closed their Billington Road washing plant in 1964. A road tipping dock facility was constructed of concrete, at this time, adjacent to the southernmost siding at Grovebury Crossing. This tipping dock remained in use until December 1969, the last regular flow of traffic going to Austin Motor Company's Longbridge factory.

Continuing sidings, Arnold's Harris Siding, Gregory Harris opened the original sand pit; Leighton Buzzard Gas Co siding; British H W Gossard & Co Ltd siding (1926); Leighton Buzzard Sand Co siding (south side of line); Also the British Rail goods depot at Grovebury Crossing.

With the rebuilding of Euston station in the mid-1960's the spoil was brought north and tipped at Grovebury. Probable closure of the last siding was December 1969.

During the 1920-30 period goods for G Allen; W Farrar; Grovebury Brickworks Ltd; Leighton Buzzard Concrete Co; Leighton Buzzard Urban District Council; Scott Brothers and F Stone would be sent to Arnold's Billington Siding.

Mr Fred Hobbs was a Signalman at Grovebury in 1959 and describes what it was like on the branch from the signalman's point of view

'I came on the railway in 1959 and went to Grovebury Crossing, my first opening was at Chelmscote Bridge an eight lever box on the main line, just before you go down to the Three Locks. But as a new signalman I was to go and learn my trade at Grovebury.

At Grovebury was the gasworks and coal yard and the sand sidings for Arnold's and Garsides. The box had the tall LNWR telegraph instruments, one side was wired to Leighton No 1 and the other side to Stanbridgeford. In between Leighton No 1 and Grovebury were two non block post boxes, Ledburn Road and Wing Road, their signalling for the 'down' was slotted to Leighton no 1 'down' branch starter at the end of no 6 platform. So when a train was signalled to us, both these crossing keepers heard it as well on their repeaters, they would then see to their gates. For the 'down' we had a distant that was situated on the opposite side of the canal. Our home signal for that was one of the old LNWR ones. When the sand empties came down he had to pull down through Billington Crossing, we then had to ring the crossing keeper to send him back and he would back into the sand siding. This would be a train of something like twenty or so empties. We had very tight clearances between the box and the wagons when they were being shunted back into the sidings.

There was a loading bridge at Billington Road where the light railway would bring the sand down and transfer it to the large standard gauge wagons.

When they came out there were two dwarf signals for another set of points that could bring them onto the 'up' line. So they would come straight out through this crossover road onto the 'up' side to return.

For Garsides trains would pick up in the afternoons. We used an Annett's Key to open this siding which we operated by inserting through a hole in the floor of the box that had a flap cover. This released the ground frame for Garsides which the Guard could then operate. When the train came out the Guard would wave his flag and we would then re-lock the points with the Annett's Key. We also had a lock in the box for the wicket gates alongside the Crossing where the pedestrians walked. All the crossings had that, it was a brown lever in the box.

A minor road into Billington before Stanbridgeford had a crossing called 'Stanbridge Mead' this was just a small cabin with no signals and no levers, just a couple of repeater instruments, it was about quarter of a mile from Stanbridgeford. There was a crossing keeper's house also at this location.

One heavy traffic was a the Dunstable parcels with box vans that ran twice daily this would be six or seven vans and brake van.

Most of the sand and chalk traffic would back up at Leighton before moving on. At about 10.30 in the morning a chalk train would come off the branch and carry straight on. Chalk empties would come onto the branch in mid afternoon heading for Totternhoe. In 1964 they were just starting to take the boxes out and I finished with the railway.'

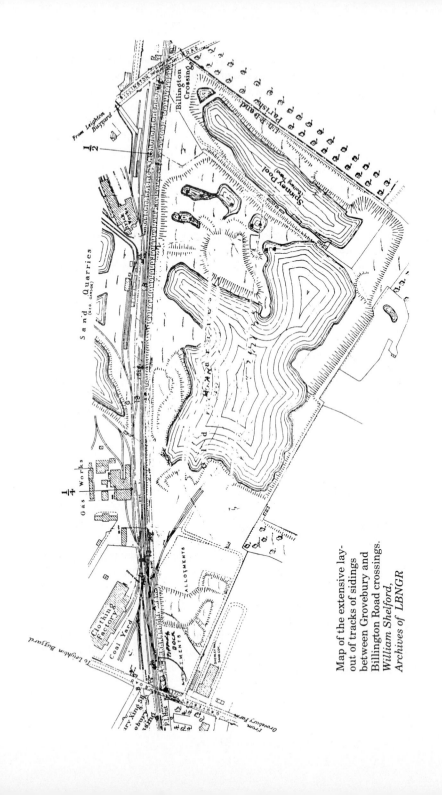

Map of the extensive lay-out of tracks of sidings between Grovebury and Billington Road crossings. *William Shelford, Archives of LBNGR*

Father and son, Arthur Pepper and Clive Pepper in Wing Crossing box
mid to late 1950's. On a higher level through the window behind are
wagons stored in Wing Goods yard,
Mrs T Pepper

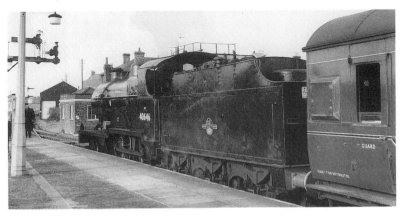

Former Midland engine 40646 just arrived at Leighton Buzzard from
Dunstable with a Stephenson Locomotive Society special on April 14, 1962
Kevin Lane

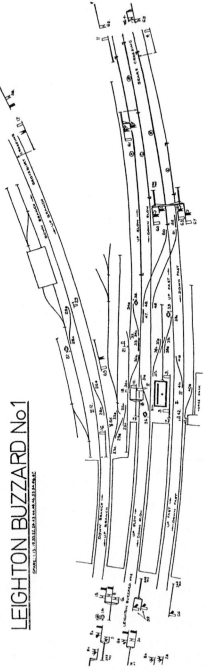

LEIGHTON BUZZARD NO 2

LEIGHTON BUZZARD No1

88

GROVEBURY CROSSING

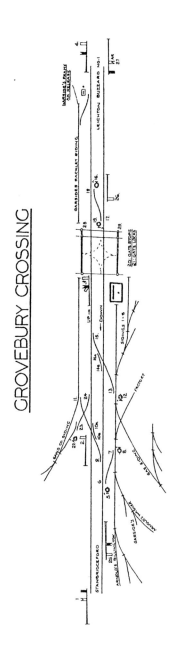

Signalbox diagrams, the branch was entered from no 2 box. Also on no 1 box diagram the additional junction between 'down' fast and 'down' slow put in by the LMS in 1927 over which the ill fated 'Royal Scot' passed in 1931. The main line box closed with electrification on July 4, 1965. The cross-over road on the Dunstable side of the signalbox was removed January 17, 1963.

89

Wing yard where much of the goods traffic was held from and to the branch, note the train of chalk waiting to go forward.
Stephen Summerson

On a dismal wet day on July 23, 1951 Webb 'Coal Tank' no 58887 prepares to propel its train to Dunstable. Of particular interest are Stephen Summerson's notes on the performance of this locomotive at this time in the chapter on locomotives.
H C Casserley

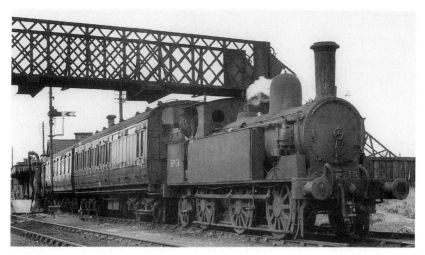

Webb 'Coal Tank' 58926 with the Dunstable train on the siding nearest the town at the station of Leighton Buzzard that abutted no 1 platform of the station in its in 1870's form.
Ken Nunn Collection, Courtesy LCGB

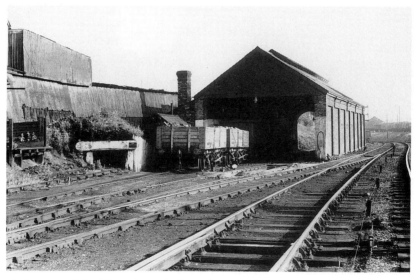

A photograph looking along the branch towards Wing yard on the higher level. On the print an 0-8-0 49287 is just visible inside the shed, presumably all other locos are out on duty. Extreme left is the short loading dock for the siding for Robert Alder's that fell out of use in the late 1950's and was used to hold a mess coach for the shed staff.
B K B Green

The locomotive shed at Leighton Buzzard that must have replaced the single road shed that was sent to Newport Pagnell in the 1880's. Clearly a restricted site for a two road shed, after an accident in 1957 the centre column was removed and the roof cut back. It was finally demolished c1962.

The locomotive steam shed seen looking south in August 1961. The wagon was for loco coal. Alongside it is the Oerlikon mess coach no M29776 on the former siding of Alder's. The distant goods shed is in Wing Yard a very necessary addition to a station hard pressed for space.The other small coach was the mess room for the carriage and wagon staff.
K C H Fairey

Leighton Buzzard station looking north in the period of the LNWR, probably early this century. The timber extended section with chamfered corners was added to the building some time after the 1880 survey. The decoration of finials along the station canopy is a curiosity for the LNWR, not noted for ornamentation, one wonders why at Leighton Buzzard. Note the ornate weighing machine in front of the lamp
Colin Holmes Collection

A train of chalk waits in one of the branch platforms, a difficult photograph to date but as the brake vans are not of the LNWR type it may be assumed that this during the period of the LMS.
Colin Holmes Collection

The siding alongside Wing Yard goods shed with timber platform and crane, the Leighton Buzzard station is in the distance.
Ian Bowley

Wing Crossing signalbox from the north side of the Wing Road in Spring 1966. This box had five levers and was the signalbox that was bought and installed at Whipsnade Zoo on July 28, 1970.
Ian Bowley

OPPOSITE PAGE: The drops from the narrow gauge to the standard gauge at Billington Road, note the crossing in background. The photograph was kindly submitted by Mr M Rudd, part of one their Company's coal wagons can be seen bottom right 'Goddard & Rudd', red with white letters shaded black. The brick work on the supporting piers look quite recent and one of the narrow gauge lines is not yet laid. Also the wagon carries the initials 'SR' which is post grouping, a guess at date would suggest mid to late 1920's.
Mr M Rudd

Seldom seen on photographs the south part of Leighton Buzzard station showing Leighton No 1 signal box and the horse and carriage landing. Note the extension to the signalbox from the LMS period, a small office for a train regulator who supported the signalman in organising the movement of trains, especially the heavy branch traffic. A regulator was sent to both boxes at Leighton from Bletchley control.
Colin Holmes Collection

A 'Super D' 0-8-0 at Grovebury Crossing.
Alan Willmott

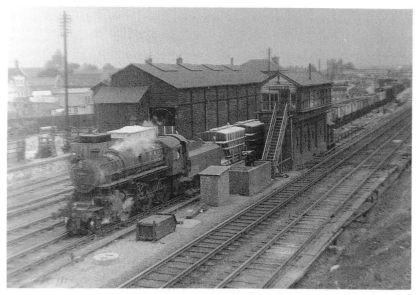

Ivatt 2-6-0 43034 passing Leighton No 2 box with the return working of
Swanbourne Sidings - Tring Cutting (Tunnel Cement Co) via Tring freight.
Note cattle pens and chalk wagon, this would almost certainly be a
'cripple' removed from a northbound train. The signal box dates from 1883,
extended in 1923.
Ian Bowley

Double headed Stanier 2-6-4 42071 and 42431 tanks pass by the entrance
to Ledburn Wharf coal yard with a special from Vauxhall Motors to
Kensington Olympia from Luton (Bute St.) via Dunstable Town and North,
Leighton, Apsley and Watford Junction on January 4, 1964.
Ian Bowley

Eight coupled LNWR goods engine arrives at Grovebury signalbox with an 'up' goods.

One of the eight coupled 'Super D's' no 48898 on the crossing at Stanbridgeford in the summer of 1952. Just visible in the mineral wagon is a load of chalk so it can be assumed that the loco is shunting Gower's Siding.
Alan Willmott

CHAPTER SIX

Stanbridgeford

The only intermediate station between the two towns of Leighton Buzzard and Dunstable situated 4¼ miles from Leighton Buzzard; it opened for passengers trains about October 1849. But did not open for goods until some time between August 1866 and October 1871. Originally the station must have been something of a rudimentary form of construction as platforms were not ordered until October 3, 1860 when it was shown in public timetables; these were surfaced with brick paviors and edged with the granite blocks first used as sleepers on the London & Birmingham Railway. The first installation was probably a siding so that goods trains could divide before ascending the incline to Dunstable, one and a quarter miles away. There is also a road crossing at this station. Another crossing further along the line towards Leighton was called Stanbridge Crossing or Stanbridge Mead. In the gatekeeper's Hut warning of the approach of trains was given by a pair of single non pegged block telegraph instruments acting as repeaters.

The station appears to have opened to serve the villages of Eaton Bray, Tilsworth, Totternhoe and Stanbridge.

The area around Stanbridge was popular for gatherings and Field Days were often held in fields alongside the station. The Leighton Buzzard Observer reported in 1919 that on a Whit Monday of glorious weather there was a huge exodus of the population of Leighton Buzzard deserting the town for country retreats on the downs. Most of the townspeople made for the local railway station for destinations to Totternhoe Knoll, Ashridge and London. The result of all this was that by evening Stanbridgeford station was literally besieged by a crowd of some 700 people returning to either Dunstable or Leighton. Many had walked from the towns but after a long day were weary and now wanted the train to go home. The Stationmaster had to call for help from Leighton to find any available coaches to make up trains for the people. A special train was then worked along the branch to disperse the people.

As S Summerson noted on October 14, 1961, 'The 1 in 40 could cause problems with slippery rails, when I photographed 8F 48646 at Dunstable it was a morning of clear Autumn sunshine but in the vale below it was thick mist. As the air was very still I could hear the train coming from a long way off, it was going very slowly and slipping repeatedly. It was a long time before it finally came into view appearing slow and laboriously over the top of the bank. Rear locomotive assistance on the climb seldom seemed to be employed with the exception of one occasion in the 1940's. Doubtless as a result of delayed traffic I saw an 0-8-0 with about thirty cattle wagons banked by another of the same class going up to Dunstable. The sound was marvellous with one-two-three-four very slowly and then repeated by the banker. Later they returned to go down as light engines coupled together and to my surprise they reappeared about an hour later and banked up another train. I never saw this repeated again.'

The last appearance of an 0-8-0 was on September 22, 1962 when 48930 worked a special passenger from Luton to Banbury and returned ascending the bank at a steady slow pace after stopping at Stanbridgeford. There was a notice at the head of the incline that read, 'Stop and pin down Brakes' .

The area had two standard gauge sidings from the branch just east of Stanbridgeford station. A lime works that was owned by Forders ran for some length; this opened in 1886 and lasted up until March 29, 1938.

Much more significant were the works of De Berenger & Gowers which opened in c1926. This siding ran to an exchange sidings, the opposite end of which the rails ran spectacularly up a steep cable worked incline of 1 in 10. Railway work at this quarry ceased about April 1965 when chalk was then pumped by pipeline. The signalbox, was little more than a ground frame, it held seven levers for working the points and 'distant' and 'home' signals, there were no ground signals as all instructions were by hand and lamp!

The chalk tippler wagons carried chalk to Rugby where it was used to make cement. The quarries were owned by Rugby Portland cement Co. Ltd. The chalk was also converted into lime. There were a number of brown side tipping wagons and green liveried former LMS brake vans. Other rolling stock were large numbers of BR chalk tipplers. There were six locomotives and a small engine shed at the bottom of the incline. The oldest engine was a Manning Wardle last steamed in October 1960 and finally broken up in 1963. There was also an Avonside Engineering loco and a Stephenson & Hawthorn, also four Sentinel 0-4-0 engines that were built for the company.

Works no.	Manufacturer	Date	Type
1995	Manning Wardle Ltd	1921	0-6-0ST
1875	Avonside (Bristol)	1921	0-4-0ST
1413	Stephenson & Hawthorn	1948	0-6-0ST
9556	Sentinel (Shrewsbury)	1953	0-4-0T
9564	Sentinel (Shrewsbury)	1954	0-4-0T
9627	Sentinel (Shrewsbury)	1957	0-4-0T

The station closed to passengers, July 2, 1962 and for Goods June 1, 1964. The last of the chalk from Totternhoe to Southam and Long Itchington (Warwickshire) was on April 15, 1965.

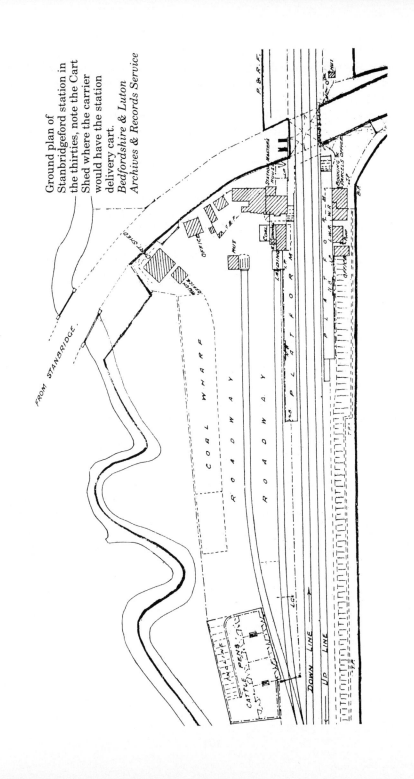

Ground plan of Stanbridgeford station in the thirties, note the Cart Shed where the carrier would have the station delivery cart. *Bedfordshire & Luton Archives & Records Service*

View of station looking east towards Dunstable on February 31, 1960
R M Casserley

Close view of a group of buildings on the 'up' side, the furthest is the booking and parcels office, the middle hut is the waiting room and the hut nearest to camera is the ladies waiting room. Note LNWR platform seat and rather puny little station sign fastened to the nameboard that would have had the station name in large bold white letters in LNWR days. This view May 26, 1956.
H C Casserley

STANBRIDGEFORD

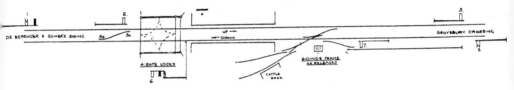

Signal box diagram for Stanbridgeford, note the long siding going in the 'up' direction towards Leighton Buzzard. This was the siding first put in in 1848 to allow trains to split before attempting Sewell Bank.
Fred Bateman

DE BERENGER & GOWER'S SIDING

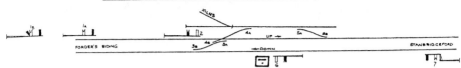

De Berenger and Gower's Siding signalbox diagram. The method of working the siding was to bring a train of empties from Leighton Buzzard, reverse into the 'up' side so that the engine could run round the train. It would then push it back onto the 'down' side. It would then go back over to the 'up' side with the guard's brake leaving this in position on the main running line whilst the engine drew out a train of full chalk wagons which it would then push up to connect with the brake. It would then go back over to the 'down' and collect the empties and push them into the chalk sidings, return, couple up to the full train and proceed to Leighton after being cleared by Stanbridgeford signal. There were no ground signals so all of this was done by hand signals and at night by hand lamp!
Fred Bateman Collection

FORDERS SIDING

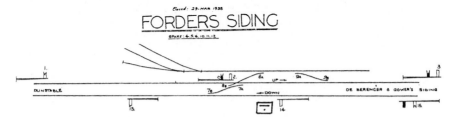

Forder Sidings signalbox diagram, for a very long siding down to a lime works .
Fred Bateman Collection

104

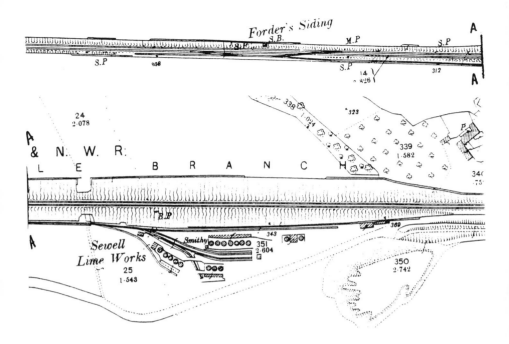

The end of the long siding to Forder's lime works on Sewell Bank which closed on March 29, 1938.
Ordnance Survey / Bedfordshire & Luton Archives & Records Service

RESTRICTED NUMBER OF VEHICLES TO BE CONVEYED BY PASSENGER TRAINS OVER CERTAIN SECTIONS OF LINE.

Section.		Up or Down.	Restricted maximum number of bogie vehicles or their equivalent. *	Remarks.
From	To			
Coalport ...	Dawley & Stirchley ...	Either	5	Trains exceeding 5 actual vehicles must have a brake vehicle at each end. In the case of a motor train the engine may be in rear.
Dawley & Stirchley ...	Hadley Junction	,,	12	
Marton Junction ...	Weedon	,,	8 for ordinary trains / 13 for mixed trains	Between Leamington Spa and Daventry.
Nottingham ...	Market Harboro' ...	,,	13	‡—Only 10 bogie vehicles or their equivalent between Shepshed and Coalville.
Shackerstone Jn. ...	Loughboro'	,,	‡13	
Banbury ...	Brackley	,,	7	
Luton (L.N.E.) ...	Dunstable	Down	10	
Dunstable ...	Leighton Buzzard ...	Up ...	†8	†—With two guards.
Leighton Buzzard ...	Dunstable	Down	†5	†—With two guards. A brake vehicle in which guard must ride must be the last vehicle of train from Stanbridgeford to Dunstable, unless an engine is in rear.
Aylesbury ...	Cheddington... ...	Either	7	

Restrictions on the Leighton - Dunstable - Luton line, the vehicles conveyed over the Dunstable - Leighton section is the same as on the line from Verney Junction to Banbury which had the gradient at Cockley Brake.

The striking feature of Totternhoe Quarries was the rope incline down to the storage sidings. This view from the top shows some full chalk wagons already lowered down. This is August 5, 1963.
Southill Collection

Storage and exchange yard looking towards the connection with the branch. A train of chalk is awaiting collection. It is remarkable to think of the enormous tonnages that were removed from here with such a rudimentary system. This view August 5, 1963
Southill Collection

Totternhoe Lime Quarries Sentinel 0-4-0TG loco no 7
Southill Collection

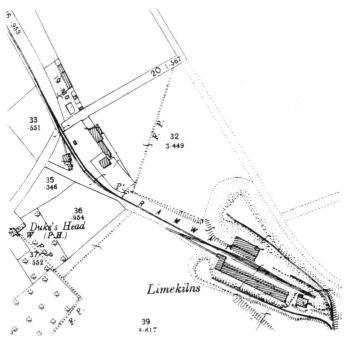

The lime kilns and cable incline in 1901.
Ordnance Survey / Bedfordshire & Luton Archives & Records Service

Mrs J Parkinson of Stanbridge is alighting from 'The Banburian' a special train (Luton - Banbury) in 1963. She was the last passenger to use Stanbridgeford station. The platform height of early unrebuilt stations is remarkably evident!
F Parkinson

An untypical locomotive a Midland Compound 4-4-0 ascends Sewell Bank towards Dunstable on April 14, 1962 to collect a special train.
Stephen Summerson

Close up view of the gates at Stanbridgeford, note the gatelamp that works through a ninety degree turn, red on one side and white on the other, this would apply as the gates were swung open to each direction appropriately
Alan Willmott

A good view along the line at Stanbridgeford as two 'Super D' engines
pass. Note the siding of the station filled with vans to collect flowers
and fruit which was very significant traffic at this station.
Alan Willmott

A cold morning in March 1959 as steam envelopes Ivatt 2-6-2T 41222 as it pauses at Dunstable with the 7.30 from Leighton Buzzard to Luton.
H C Casserley

CHAPTER SEVEN

Dunstable

The first station opened June 1, 1848 at Dunstable was a simple affair but a significant one as the station received 8,263 tons of coal in the following six months of the year. The station had opened for goods on the previous May 29. The rails ran up to the A5 trunk road that passed by at an angle to the railway on the same level. In 1861 to increase facilities cattle pens were removed from Claydon on the Bletchley to Oxford line and brought to Dunstable.

The situation became more contentious when the line came in from the east supported by the GNR who were in favour of a joint station. The LNWR requested that a new station at Dunstable be built by the GNR. However the extension of the line required a bridge to be built over the A5 which was done by completely rebuilding the Dunstable station on a higher level and reducing the road level a few feet to gain clearance. The new passenger station was opened in January 1866.

The GNR did gain some advantage from their own station at Dunstable Church Street in that it was more convenient than the LNWR for the town. It had a wooden platform. A serious fire destroyed much of the station in 1870.

A siding at the top of the incline running from the station was put in requested by a Mr Rowe in 1902. This was the Dunstable Lime Company's siding. Later other companies had connections to it, the Bedfordshire County Council and the Midland Tar Distillers, the latter brought many tar wagons onto the branch.

There may well have been locomotive facilities at Dunstable from 1848 when little was available at Leighton and the branch was worked to a terminus at Dunstable, but this would in all probability cease with the continuation of the line to Luton.

Preceding the station is a local road crossing where the station signalbox was positioned. This was a type 4 LNWR box that remained until the signalling was altered and a new box installed called Dunstable North on August 16, 1958. There had been some subsidence affecting the old box and with the new box it was possible to bring the gasworks siding into the box instead of being worked from a ground frame.

Instruments for the working of the electric staff section between Dunstable and Luton were housed in the station buildings. The working was 'down' to Dunstable and 'up' to Hatfield and 'up' to Leighton.

The line to Luton remained open to passengers until April 26, 1965. Sidings on the GNR side were for Associated Portland Cement Manufacturers Ltd, Bagshaw & Co, Waterlow & Sons and Blows Down Siding. The station closed to goods on October 9, 1967. Cement and oil traffic continued until 1988.

The story of railway connection to Dunstable may as yet be without a conclusion as there is still a very strong case for the line between Dunstable and Luton to be reopened. A report in the Dunstable & District Citizen mentioned a major survey to assess support for passenger trains between Dunstable and Luton. British Rail estimated it would cost £5-7million. At the time of writing the track is still in situ between Dunstable and Luton.

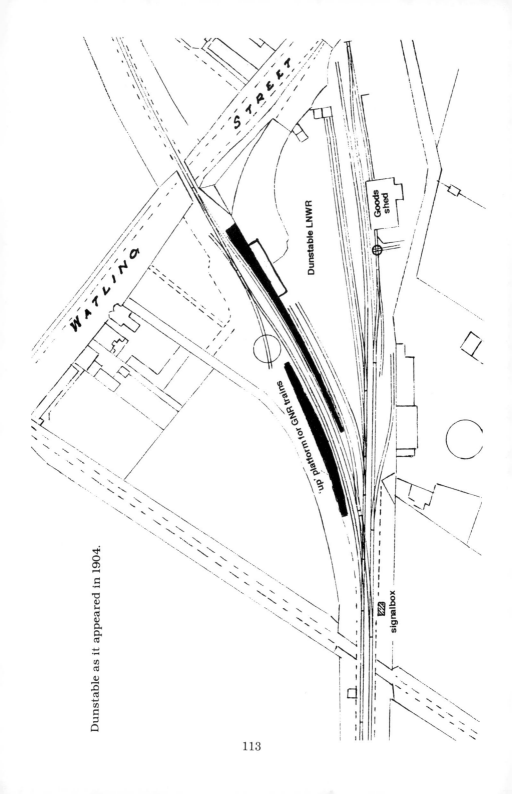

Dunstable as it appeared in 1904.

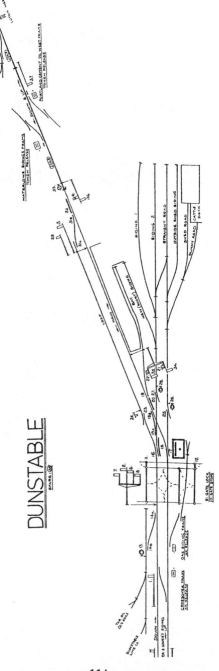

Dunstable signalbox diagram in LMS/BR note repositioning of gas works siding compared to the LNWR plan of 1902.
Fred Bateman Collection

114

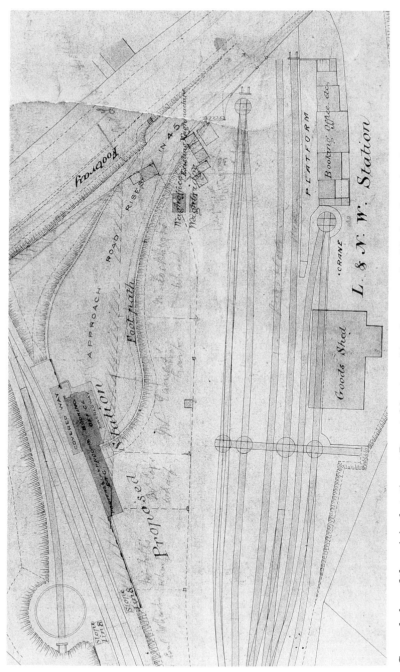

Ground plan of the original station at Dunstable at road level compared with the plans for the new station to be elevated with bridge over the A5 road for line to Luton. Note goods shed siding of original station, the run round is facilitated by using a wagon turntable, a slow process probably using horses.
Bedfordshire & Luton Archives & Records Service

Leighton Buzzard push-pull train arrives at Dunstable in the 1950's.
Stephen Summerson

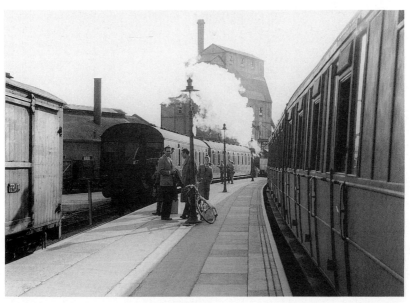

Dunstable North with Leighton Buzzard - Dunstable push-pull train in the charge of 2MT 2-6-2T. The former LNER coach on the right is of a Welwyn bound train. Note fruit van on left in bay for branch.
Alan Willmott

View along the platform in the direction of Luton in June 1959
Alan Willmott

Bright sunshine greets the exertions of 2-8-0 48446 ascending Sewell Bank towards Dunstable on October 14, 1961. Elsewhere in this book Stephen Summerson describes the moment as he heard the unseen locomotive begin its challenge of the incline, a sound filling the distances for many miles around. The 2-8-0's always worked up the bank tender first. Note the empty tar tank wagons next to the engine bound for the Midland Tar Distillers at Dunstable.
Stephen Summerson.

The bridge between two great railway companies, former LNWR station off right, from where an N7 0-6-2T crosses the A5 road. Note the road lowered beneath the bridge to gain clearance. Period cars of 1959 pass by, a Ford Prefect and an MG saloon followed by a distant Sunbeam Talbot.

Dunstable GNR that became Dunstable Town station, rebuilt after the fire
of 1870.
F A Blencowe

View from the end of the platform at Dunstable Town looking towards
Dunstable North in the 1960's. Visible is the siding for Waterlow's.
Bedfordshire & Luton Archives & Records Service

L. M. S.

Week Days only.	a.m	p.m	p.m	p.m	p.m	Notes.
LUTON, L.N.E. ... dep	8 30	12 45	5 45	7 55		A Leighton
Dunstable, L.M.S. ,,	8 46	1 16	6 10	8 15		B. arr. 10.44.
Leighton Buzz'd arr.	9 1	1 31	6 27	8 30		B Sats. 12.35.
Bletchley dep.	9 11	1 42	6 42	8 52		C Sats. 12.47.
Oxford, L.M.S. arr.	9 21	1 52	6 53	9 2		D Sats. 3.47.
	...	1 17	6 34	...	11 13	e Sats.
Bletchley ... dep.	9 45	2 0	7 35	9 8		excepted.
Wolverton ... arr.	9 54	2 9	7 45	9 17		F Sats. 7.8.
Northampton § ... ,,	10 30	2 34	8 P12	9 41		G Sats. 1.40.
Birmingham† ,,	10 96	3 4	10 18	12 40		H Arr. Bletch-
Bletchley ...dep.	9 45	2 0	8 35	9 8		ley 9.13.
Crewe ...arr.	1 15	6 2	10 56	5 L4		K Mondays
Liverpool,Lime St. ,,	2 55	7 10	12 43	6 130		Crewe 5.16,
						Bletchley
Week Days only.	a.m	a.m	a.m	a.m	p.m	7.54.
Liverpool ... dep	12 2	12 30	8 0	0 1145	2 0	L Sun.morns.
Crewe ... ,,	1 32	7 K5	9 5	1 83	3 13	5.0.
Bletchley ... arr.	4 50	A9K57	11 38	304	16 41	N Sats. 7.19.
Birmingham†d.	...	7H30	8 45	2 37	3 25	P Sats. 8.5.
Northampton§	4 23	9 0	...	4 156	1	Q Sats. 7.30.
Wolverton ,,	...	9 41	...	4 406	32	R Sats. 7.39.
Bletchley arr.	4 50	945	10 39	4 496	41	s Sats. only
Oxford dep.		6 25	10 28	2 405	0	† Sun.morns.
Bletchley ,,	7 10	7 51	1853	5 127	0	6.53.
Leighton B. arr.	7 21	8 2	2 C3	5 247	12	New Street.
dep.	7 30	...	1264	5 307	40	§ Castle.
Dunstable ,,	7 46	...	1810	5 475	6 56	
LUTON, L.N.E. arr.	8 6	...	1810	6 398	34	

HOBBS' LUTON TIME TABLE

(66TH YEAR.)
and Insurance £250 Ticket.

Printed and published by T. G. Hobbs, 28, Cheapside

No. 783]. DECEMBER, 1945. [3d

Services shown are as advertised by the various Companies, but are subject to alteration without notice.

Head Post Office. Hours :—Week Days, 8.30 to 6.30. Sundays, 9.0 to 10.30 a.m.

	a.m.	p.m.
London & Suburban	12.15	
Harpenden, St. Albans and District...		12.15
Dunstable & Leighton	5.0	
Luton	6.0	
London & Suburban	9.15	
Cambridge, Leicester, Watford ...	10.0	
London, Hitchin, Letchworth ...	11.0	
Aylesbury, Bedford, Bletchley, Harpenden, Leighton Buz., Northampton, St. Albans, N., E., N.W., Midlands, Scotland	11.45	
‡ Not Mons.		

London, S. and W. of Eng. and S. Wales...12.30
Dunstable 1.15
London, Foreign and General ... 2.30
Midlands 3.30
London & Suburban, Mid. and N.W. Eng., N. Wales, West of England ... 4.45
General Night Mail ... 6.0
London & Suburban, E., S. and W. of Eng., and S. Wales ... 8.15

Sundays. { London 6.30 p.m { General 8.15 ,, ... 9.0

W. BENNETT, Head Postmaster.

B. E. BARRETT, LTD.,

Motor Engineers :: Haulage Contractors :: Car Agents.

CASTLE STREET, LUTON.

OPEN DAY AND NIGHT.

'Phone: Luton 846 PBx.

120

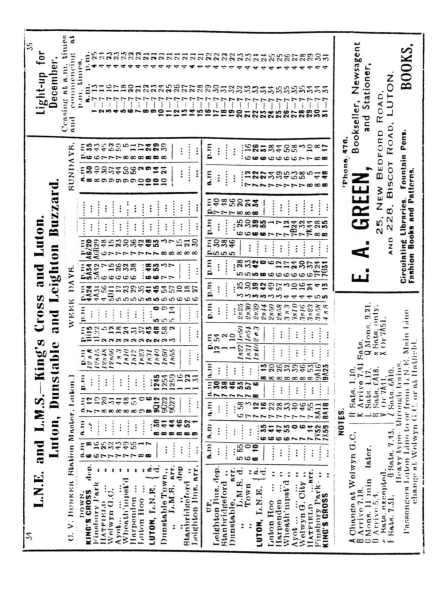

Hobb's timetable in December 1945.
Stephen Summerson

121

One of the heavier 0-6-2T N2 with mineral wagons awaiting clearance for the single line section to Luton from Dunstable North on September 24, 1955.
H C Casserley

DUNSTABLE.

Coaching vehicles 57 ft. in length and 9 ft. 4 ins. in width over projections, must not work into the bay platform line and the disused platform.

One of the N7 class no 69698 shunting at Luton (Bute Street).
R A S

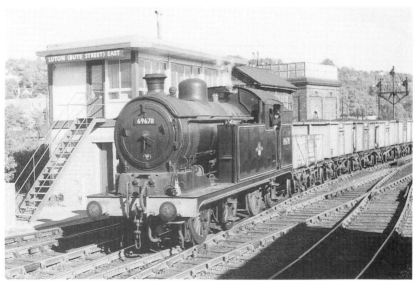

A train of coal at Luton hauled by N7 0-6-0 no 69678.
R A S

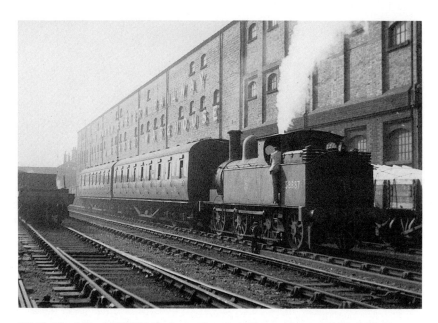

Webb 'Coal Tank' 58887 that wandered on lines all around Bletchley as now entered former Great Northern territory as it waits at Luton (Bute Street) on July 7, 1952. The engine is waiting to propel the 8.30 am Luton to Leighton Buzzard into the platform having crossed to the 'down' line
Stephen Summerson

LIST OF SINGLE LINES OF RAILWAY.

Single lines of Railway worked by Train Staff and Ticket.

Section V of the Rule Book.

Section of line.	Shape of staff.	Colour of staff.	Staff stations.	Persons appointed to receive staff or ticket from, and deliver it to, the driver.
Littleworth Extension Railway	Round ...	Black ...	{ Littleworth Junction, Cross Keys Junction	Signalman. Signalman.
Leighswood Branch	,, ...	Red ...	{ Leighswood sidings, Aldridge Colliery No. 2 Weighbridge	Signalman or shunter Shunter.
Dunstable (L.M.S.) and Luton .(L.N.E.)	Square ...	Steel ...	{ Luton (L.N.E.) ... ... Dunstable	Station master or porter.
Aylesbury Branch	Round ...	Red ...	{ Aylesbury ... ... Cheddington	Signalman. Signalman, station master or foreman.

Lines worked by electric train staff and ticket.

Stanier 8F with Fowler tender shunts the yard at Dunstable on September 11, 1963.
Southill Collection

RESTRICTED NUMBER OF VEHICLES TO BE CONVEYED BY PASSENGER TRAINS OVER CERTAIN SECTIONS OF LINE.

Section. From	To	Up or Down.	Restricted maximum number of bogie vehicles or their equivalent. *	Remarks.
Coalport	Dawley & Stirchley	Either	5	⎫ Trains exceeding 5 actual vehicles must
Dawley & Stirchley	Hadley Junction	,,	12	⎬ have a brake vehicle at each end. In the case of a motor train the engine may be in rear.
Marton Junction	Weedon	,,	8 for ordinary trains 13 for mixed trains	⎫⎬⎭ Between Leamington Spa and Daventry.
Nottingham	Market Harboro'	,,	13	—
Shackerstone Jn.	Loughboro'	,,	‡13	‡—Only 10 bogie vehicles or their equivalent between Shepshed and Coalville.
Banbury	Brackley	,,	7	—
Luton (L.N.E.)	Dunstable	Down	10	—
Dunstable	Leighton Buzzard	Up	7	—
			† 8	†—With two guards.
Leighton Buzzard	Dunstable	Down	7	—
			† 8	†—With two guards. A brake vehicle in which guard must ride must be the last vehicle of train from Stanbridgeford to Dunstable, unless an engine is in rear.
Aylesbury	Cheddington	Either	7	—

—Three six-wheeled vehicles count as two eight-wheeled vehicles.

Restriction for number of vehicles on the line.

Into the diesel age as D5640 in early British Railways two tone green with the 5.13 pm from Welwyn meets 2-6-2T with the 6.05pm to Leighton Buzzard at Dunstable on April 14, 1962.
H C Casserley

View from the opposite side of the bridge looking towards Dunstable North through the window of Craven's DMU E51298 on September 11, 1963.
Southill Collection

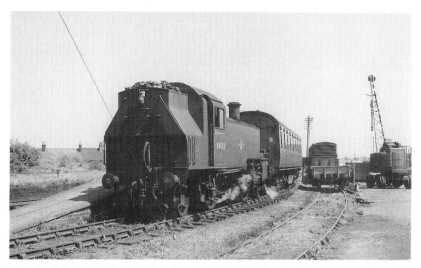

Standard 2-6-2T 84002 on Leighton Buzzard to Dunstable push-pull at Dunstable.
Stephen Summerson

Seen from the crossing a Standard 2-6-2T leaves as 'Super D' waits with coaching stock.
R A S

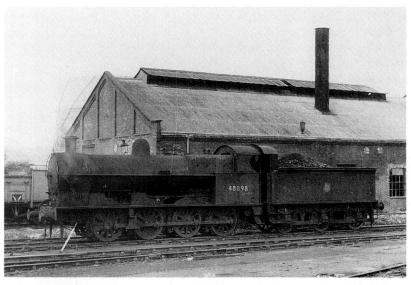

'Super D' 48898 with cab fixtures on tender shunts the yard at Dunstable on May 26, 1956.
H C Casserley

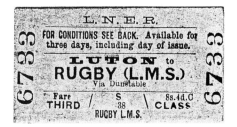

OPPOSITE PAGE: Eastern Region meets Midland Region at Dunstable North station, Stanier 2-6-4T 42591 on the 6.10pm for Leighton Buzzard and N7 0-6-2T 69648 has arrived from Hitchin and Luton on June 29, 1953.

Class 31 diesel approaching from Luton to Dunstable Town on June 25, 1962
F A Blencowe

A Bury 2-2-2 locomotive of the 1840's.

CHAPTER EIGHT

Engines in use on the Branch

In 1889 a single road steam shed was taken from Leighton Buzzard and installed at Newport Pagnell; this was subsequently destroyed by fire in 1916. The situation at Leighton had been developing steadily to need more engines for the freight traffic that was required along the branch to Dunstable and Luton. Although the survey for 1880 shows a two road shed in situ at Leighton which would be the one on the photographs with the curved arch entrances, this would have followed on from the redevelopment in the early 1850's. Full use was made of a restricted site with two roads making the clearances at the entrances very tight, a matter of inches, replacing a smaller single road building there subsequent to the 1859 development. After the accident of 1957, when a fireman was killed the centre column and part of the roof was cut back giving greater clearance.

The branch proved a severe testing ground for early engines, the inheritance of the London & Birmingham were the little bar-framed Bury engines 0-4-0 and 2-4-0 with 5ft 9in driving wheels which were hard put to work this branch. Two engines with 4ft driving wheels were built to specially run this line, these were 0-4-0 type nos 172 and 173. Later conversions of Allen tender engines converted to side tanks were brought onto the line in 1873 one named 'Gorgon' originally built in 1847, then rebuilt as a 2-4-0 side tank with a wheelbase of 4ft 8$^{1}/_{2}$ inches by 7ft 4 inches. Weight 26 tons 11cwt two cylinders of 15$^{1}/_{4}$ inches x 20 inches. This was rebuilt about 1863. The other loco 'Giant' was built in 1853 with straight frames. These were used to run the timetable with a train formation of a third class brake carriage; a composite carriage and another third class brake carriage, at that time almost certainly four-wheel stock. Later, in 1892 a 2-4-0 tank no 1191 of 38 tons came onto the line and the train was increased to five vehicles. These were a third class brake, two composites, a third class carriage and another third class brake. All four-wheelers each with a 15ft wheelbase except the third carriage which was a wheelbase of 12ft 10 inches.

Through trains between Leighton Buzzard and Luton were usually handled in LNWR days by Webb 0-6-2T 'Coal Tanks' which were sent new to Dunstable shed. The very modestly designed 5ft 6inches 2-4-2T, with a push-pull set designed for branch line work were also allocated to this line, which must have been very testy for them. Later in BR days the Ivatt 2-6-2T continued with the push-pull set. The goods work must have been tough going with small engines as it proved to be no simple matter with the generations of eight coupled locos of the LNWR. These locomotives had to be worked at full gear and it was a feature of the district to hear them working up the gradients of the branch from remarkably far off. Engines of this type seen on the branch were 48930, 49094 and 49403 all from Leighton shed. Bletchley also provided nos 49021, 49314, 48927 and 49430. Seen also on the branch was former Midland 4F 44397 with a train of coal and agricultural produce. 'Coal Tanks' Working the branch in British Railways days were 58887 and 58926. One diesel was seen on the branch by railway historian Fred Cockman, no D5610 on April 22, 1961. Owing to the slump in trade in the north in the 1930's, Lancashire & Yorkshire Railway 0-6-0's were used on the branch, that were nicknamed 'Gracie Fields'. These were nos 12107, 12105, 12108, 12086.

During World War II Stephen Summerson, noted the following; 'During 1941-42 the passenger workings were in the charge of 2-4-2T no 6683 and 0-6-2T's nos 7763, 7797. Goods work was in the charge of 0-8-0's nos 9127/8/31/8/93/6, 9201/13, 9408/9/16 and 8917.

The following year 1943, passenger workings were hauled by 0-6-2T 7830. This engine was renumbered 27830 in February 1945 until it was withdrawn in 1949 the only one of the later numbered engines to be given a 20000 number. It was at Bletchley throughout and often worked the branch. In 1944 6604 2-4-2T and 7773 0-6-2T were to be seen working the branch. On the 6th June 1945 2-4-2T 6683 was seen; and in 1946 on the 6th of April 2-4-2T 6683 was seen again. In 1947, the final year of the LMS, during January

27561 was the engine in charge but by September 1, 2-4-2T 6912 had assumed the role.

There was a constant procession of 0-6-2T 'Coal Tanks' and 2-4-2T as a result of transfers and withdrawals. With the arrival of a non fitted push-pull engine such as 6604 and 6912, the train halted outside Dunstable North and the engine ran round to propel the coaches into the platform. I recall this happening with 'Watford' tanks 6883, 6909 and 6912/36 that were present only in 1946 and 1948.

I witnessed a prodigious feat of haulage by the branch engine no 7742 one day in 1945. The engine was summoned from its usual role to take charge of a failed Blackpool express, its 'Jubilee' loco had knocked off its right hand cylinder cover. The loco was to continue with the train from Leighton Buzzard to Bletchley. I was at the north end of Linslade Tunnel and was astounded to see 7742 emerge on the 'down' slow working flat out and doing about ten miles and hour hauling the 'Jubilee' and its ten coach train. About an hour later it returned light engine to its normal duties!

Number 58887 was the last LNWR engine to work the passenger trains and its final branch workings to my knowledge were in the week ending October 17, 1954.

The first Ivatt 2-6-2T to arrive was 41222 which came to Bletchley on September 10, 1949.

Two Standard 2-6-2T nos 84002/4 came to Bletchley in early August 1956. On the last day of passenger working June 30, 1962 84002 worked the morning train to Luton and back and then 41222 freshly painted after overhaul, ran the mid-day and tea time trips.

The Monday to Friday passenger service working through from Welwyn and Luton saw various N7 0-6-2's working the trains into Leighton Buzzard. Also English Electric type 1's were used in the summer of 1959 but as they did not have steam heating equipment they were removed with the onset of winter and replaced with N7 engines. That was until sufficient Brush type 2's became available and they ran the service until closure. The former LNWR 0-8-0's were partially displaced by Stanier 2-8-0's and by June 1962 they had finished on the branch entirely. The preserved 'Coal Tank' served a year at Bletchley from late 1949 until late 1950 as 58926 and I noted it on the branch passenger service in 1950.'

The water columns were cut off at Leighton station on April 15, 1962; the shed itself was officially closed on November 5, 1962.

The Standard 2-6-2T no 84004 an engine of the Bletchley branches seen on
the turntable at Bletchley in the late 1950's.They were often turned at
Bletchley before working the Dunstable branch so that they would be
smokebox first. Historical modellers note, the hut on the left used as mess
cabin by loco fire raisers, also sludge tender on right.
Mr G J Arrow

A G2A 0-8-0 goods locomotive for which the Dunstable branch became its metier. Hard working and reliably efficient in experienced hands they seldom failed. One locoman that worked on these engines from Bletchley described them thus. 'With a lb a wagon on the steam pressure and as long as you have enough water to cover the bottom nut on the water gauge a 'Super D' will keep going'. This loco was introduced in February 1918, rebuilt in September 1944 and finally withdrawn in November 1962. Historical modellers note the totem on the tender facing to the rear.
Stephen Summerson

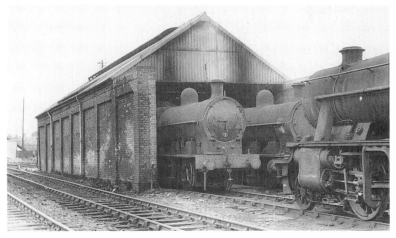

Goods engines at Leighton Buzzard shed August 7 1961. Note the cut back of the shed roof and removal of the centre pillar following the tragic accident of 1957.
K C H Fairey

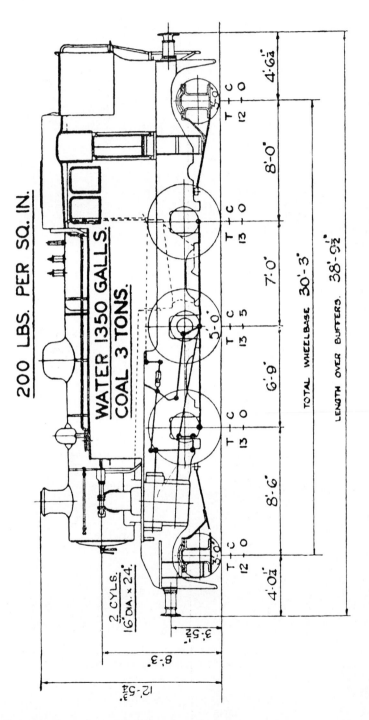

The Ivatt 2-6-2T introduced in 1946 for light branch line work. They ran along with the Standard 2-6-2T in the last flourish of branch line days. Bletchley had at least two 41222 and 41275 and they were to be found going to Aylesbury, Bedford, Buckingham, Newport Pagnell and Dunstable.

Fred Bateman Collection

Stations	sched	time	speed	time	speed	time	speed
Luton Bute Street	0			0		0	
DunstableT *arr*				8.56		9.57	
dep	11			10.09		10.35	
Dunstable N *arr*	14			12.37		13.26	
dep	0			0		0	
1 in 40			41		42		35
Stanbridge *arr*		4,41		4.48		5.35	
dep	6	6.22		5.25		6.16	
			54		55		49
Leighton B *arr*	15	12.38		11.56		13.35	
DATE		April 8, 1951		July 30, 1952		Aug. 22, 1952	
ENGINE		58887		41275		58887	

Stations	sched	time	speed
Leighton B	0	0	
Stanbridge *arr*		7.36	
dep	8	8.21	
1 in 40 foot			39
top			19
Dunstable N	16	14.20	
DATE	AUGUST 8, 1951		
ENGINE	58887		

In 1951/2 I did some timing with some of the branch passenger trains. The speeds down the 1 in 40 were very good by the 'Coal Tank' which sometimes went to 49 to 54 mph. As can be seen it was still on 19mph at the top of the climb on a 'down' run. The 2-4-2 tank engine with 5' 6" driving wheels made much harder work of it.
Stephen Summerson

137

Webb 'Coal Tank' no 7773 at Leighton Buzzard in 1948. Introduced by the
LNWR as no 570 in 1887 it became 7773 in 1922 and subsequently went
on to become British Railways 58919. It was withdrawn in 1939 but was a
year later re-introduced to continue working up until December 1952.
Stephen Summerson

The Webb 'Coal Tank' no 58887 departs from Stanbridgeford for
Dunstable in 1949.
Stephen Summerson

Index

Other railway titles by the same author published by
LAMPLIGHT PUBLICATIONS

The Banbury to Verney Junction Branch (176pp)
The story of the LNWR/LMS branch of over twenty-one miles to
Banbury from Verney Junction on the Oxford - Cambridge line passing
through Padbury, Buckingham and Brackley. This is related with over
one hundred photographs and many maps and diagrams and captures
well the atmosphere of the country railway.

The Wolverton to Newport Pagnell Branch (144pp)
This concerns a branch of just under four miles but very busily worked
with trains of workmen going to and from Wolverton works and school
children. Calling at Bradwell and Great Linford stations on the way.
The very many photographs include views from early days of the
LNWR and the works that produced such outstanding perfections of
the coach builder's skill. The line and its attendant train the 'Newport
Nobby' was very affectionately regarded by the locals that used it
which is evidently portrayed.

A History of the Railways of Oxfordshire part 1 (The North)
(192pp)
The first of this two part history of the railways of the county
showing all lines north of Oxford including the GWR, LNWR and
GCR. There are also many contributions from people that worked on
the railways and industries alongside which provides a unique
perception of industrial life that is now a part of history.

Lamplight Publications
260 Colwell Drive, Witney, Oxon OX8 7LW
and
38 Spinney Drive, Cherwell Heights, Banbury,
Oxon OX16 9TA